Sin Makes You Stupid
There's a better way to live!

By Kevin Shorkey

Visit us at our website:
www.sinmakesyoustupid.com

Free Small Group Resources are Available
on our Website

Bible Quotes are from the NIV and ESV

ISBN: 1489587144
ISBN-13: 9781489587145

dedication: To Rod and Edie Ward:

Their friendship has been life changing for my wife Sheila and me. We have shared much laughter and great joy together. God uses them to lift us up when we are sinking from the difficulties of life. They have reached down into the pit of discouragement and helped us see Christ in the most painful of situations. The active constant in their lives is Jesus. Friends like these are rare – We are deeply blessed!

Table of Contents

EPILOGUE

A successful business man known for his exceptional ability to make the right decisions at critical moments becomes addicted to gambling. He loses his home and business. Was he thinking that his losses wouldn't catch up to him?

A brilliant financial manager is under pressure to be more successful this year than last. He falsifies his portfolio and exaggerates his earnings. His clients get the bad news when they see his arrest on television. Did he really believe that he wouldn't get caught someday?

A super talented and very popular Hollywood star is caught up in the party scene. She spends years bouncing from the courtroom to rehab. Her fans forget her talent and see her only as a tabloid personality. How could she fool herself and become convinced that drugs and alcohol would enhance her career? A pastor who has served in ministry for 35 years gets tangled up in an immoral relationship with a woman in his church. When he is found out, he loses his wife, the respect of his children, his ministry and many of his friends. He then has to explain himself to people who inquire about why he left the pastorate. His sin follows him the rest of his life. As a pastor, he had dealt with people who's sin caught up with them. Was he really persuaded that no one would ever know?

Intelligent gifted people trading the best things in their lives for those of lesser value. What were they thinking? Sin turns smart people stupid!

Steven Mulhall appeared before Broward County Circuit Court Judge Michael Orlando on February 23, 2012 for a parole hearing.

Police allege that on his way out of the courtroom, Mulhall took the Judge's name placard off the door.

The police's evidence?

Mulhall apparently posted photos of himself holding the stolen placard on his girlfriend's Facebook page.

"The nameplate is like only $40, not that big of a crime, but what an idiot. He puts it on facebook," Broward County Sheriff Al Lamerti told the Sun Sentinel.

He violated the terms of his parole by stealing, from a judge he appeared before no less. He's got multiple convictions for petty theft, so now there is a felony."

WHAT WAS HE THINKING?

World Magazine

Chapter 1
Sin Turns Smart People Stupid!

My wife Sheila was taught by her dad that she was accountable to God. She has never viewed this as oppressive or limiting but as protective and freeing. I was living against God when I met her and yet was very attracted to her.

First dates are usually filled with careful conversation designed to show the best side of ourselves. My first date with Sheila began with a blunt and honest conversation before we were even out of her driveway.

"I know what kind of guy you are."

"Really?"

"Yes, and I'm not that kind of girl, so why don't I just get out of the car and go back in the house."

"I want to go out with you because you are different than any woman I've ever met. I don't know what it is but there is something about you that's different."

"That's God."

We went out and I learned that God was not the supernatural oppressor of happiness. I discovered that I could trust Him with me.

I began to understand that God's knowing me was a good thing. Accountability can be preventative. A protective filter to help you see sin for what it is, recognize its tug on your soul and turn to God for the strength to say, 'No'.

God had just given the Israelites their first great victory as they entered the Promised Land of Canaan. They didn't even have to fight! After marching around the city of Jericho once a day for six days and seven times on the seventh day; God flattened the walls! An amazing miracle that showed both the Israelites and their enemies the unmatchable power of God's hand working on behalf of His people. I would like to have been at that victory party – imagine the praise and worship they must have had!

The victory was short lived because someone messed up. God had commanded the Israelites not to take any valuables from Jericho for themselves. These things were to go in the Lord's treasury. But Achan took some things anyway – in spite of the warning of destruction for those who disobeyed.

What was he thinking? Did he really believe that God wouldn't know?

"What was I thinking?" I have said these words to myself after doing something stupid. The 'What was I thinking?' question often hits us immediately after we have sinned. We have a natural fear of being found out quickly. The fear tends to subside as time goes by and we assume no one knows. We begin to relax as we realize that we are getting away with sin. We have outsmarted everyone and we are pretty sure that God doesn't know what happened either. 'What was I thinking?' becomes 'I got away with it!'.

Achan may have felt this way after hiding the silver, gold and a really nice cloak under his tent. In his lust he missed something very important: he ignored the **God Factor**.

What was he thinking? The Israelites were breaking camp and moving on a regular basis. His lust for wealth made him shortsighted. He would have to dig up the stuff every time Israel moved – and then he would have to hide it again.

Did he really believe that his sin would not affect the entire nation as God had warned? The Israelites lost their next battle because of Achan's sin. When Joshua cried out to God in defeat God told him that sin in the camp had caused the Israelites to lose the battle.

The next day Joshua, under God's direction, gathered the Israelites together and began the sin discovery process. As he cast lots to discover which tribe contained the offender, Achan must have had a sense that his secret was vulnerable. When the process continued; narrowing the scope down to clans, he had to be squirming. Finally, Achan's family was chosen and he was called forward and confessed. The consequence – death.

Achan's sin cost him everything. His sin made him stupid. As he was being executed I bet he said to himself, 'What was I thinking?'

Achan's sin had deep roots. I know that because of the huge risk he took. He must have been toying with a strong desire to have wealth. He was consumed to the point where he couldn't see the potential consequences. He had the ability to figure out how to conceal and carry nearly fifty pounds of gold plus some silver and a flashy robe. He had to be pretty smart to pull this off. And yet was not smart enough to evaluate what could happen to him and his family if he was caught. Smart and yet stupid at the same time – sin does that to you.

Achan learned some valuable lessons too late because he ignored the **God Factor**.

God has a discovery process when it comes to sin. Achan saw it coming and did nothing. Maybe he thought he was too smart to get caught. Maybe he was hoping against hope that the blame would land on someone else. Or perhaps he didn't think it could happen to him.

What is the **God Factor**?

God knows everything about you. He knows what you are thinking and doing, as well as what you are thinking about doing. Check out the language King David uses in Psalm 139. I have emphasized the words he uses about God's attentiveness towards us:

> [1] You have **searched** me, LORD,
> and you **know** me.
> [2] You **know** when I sit and when I rise;
> you **perceive** my thoughts from afar.
> [3] You **discern** my going out and my lying down;
> you are **familiar** with all my ways.
> [4] Before a word is on my tongue
> you, LORD, **know it completely**.
> [5] You **hem me in** behind and before,
> and you **lay your hand upon me**.

⁶ Such knowledge is too wonderful for me,
too lofty for me to attain.

Consider the flow of this passage about God's aware-ness. Each verse expands on the previous to give us the whole picture of God's attentiveness to us.

Verse 1- He searches – He watches our lives closely.

Verse 2 – He perceives – He has wise understanding.

Verse 3 – He discerns – He scrutinizes our ways. He is deeply familiar with how we think and feel; our strengths and weaknesses, and even our tendencies.

Verse 4 – He knows us completely. To the point where He hears our words while they are still thoughts. He knows what we really think even when we don't say it!

Verse 5 – He hems us in – He surrounds us with Himself!

The moment Achan entertained thoughts of stealing; God had already caught him!

Could he hide from God or escape through cunning and deceit? Is anyone able to escape the grasp of God?

King David asked this question already knowing the answer, "Where can I go from Your Spirit? Where can I flee from Your presence?" (:7).

The answer is obvious – nowhere.

That's the **God Factor**!

When it comes to sin we tend to have a wrong perspective. We think that fooling people is all we have to do to get away clean. Joshua didn't know about Achan's sin. He was completely fooled until God revealed the truth to him. God was not fooled!

King David sees accountability as a positive, protective and preventative tool to be used regularly in our lives. At the end of Psalm 139 he accepts and appreciates God's attentiveness to him.

> Search me, O God, and know my heart; test me and know my anxious thoughts.
> See if there is any offensive way in me, and lead me in the way everlasting. :23-24

ACTION POINTS

1. What are you hiding under your tent? God already sees it. Why don't you dig it up and show it to Him yourself? Be proactive with confession.

2. Are you ignoring God's presence surrounding you? You are more vulnerable to sin when you do not practice daily accountability to God. Did you know that Jesus intercedes for you 24/7 before his Father's throne? Believers can bring anything to Him and he will give help as we need it.

3. Memorize Psalm 139:23-24 as a daily accountability prayer to God.

4. Invite God to work on you, in you, through you and with you. Become the person He created you to be.

✳ ✳ ✳

FOR SMALL GROUP DISCUSSION

1. What harm was caused as a result of Achan's sin?
   To himself
   To his family
   To the Israelite soldiers and their families

2. Read Luke 12:1-3 and 1John 1:9

3. Is it important to feel a sense of accountability to God?

4. What are some ways we can correct sin before it is found out? Discuss the importance of being pro-active.

In April of 2012 a group of United States Secret service agents were in Cartegena, Columbia preparing for a visit by President Obama.

An agent met a female 'escort' at a bar and took her back to his hotel room. At the bar, she claims that she told him the evening with her would cost $800. She said that he agreed.

The next morning the deal broke down and the Secret Service agent offered her $30. She pressed him to pay what he had agreed to pay. He told her to leave his room.

Another 'escort' who was across the hall with a Secret Service agent heard her crying. Both women tried to get the man to pay up.

On her way out of the hotel she came across a police officer in the hallway. He became involved and a hotel security person showed up as well.

The 'escort' finally settled for $225 and left.

News of the dispute hit the media.

Twelve Secret Service agents were relieved of their duties. They have returned home disgraced. Some are married men.

I wouldn't want to be in their homes explaining the situation to their wives.

Walking into this sin was easy. But it isn't easy now!

Chapter 2
The Path to Stupid Goes Downhill

I was standing on the rim of the Grand Canyon. Someone suggested we go down the trail. I said, 'Cool!' and off we went. After following the path on the canyon wall for a while we came upon a sign. It was there to warn us that it takes a lot longer to go up than it took going down. It also stated that hikers needed to stay hydrated for our own safety. I glanced at my 20 oz. bottle of water and continued down the trail. Sometime later, about an hour into the walk, we came upon another sign stating the same warning. Someone in our group (much wiser than me) strongly recommended that we head back to the top. We all agreed. I noticed that I had consumed all of my water on the way down. I wasn't worried, 'How hard could it be going back up? After all,' I reasoned, 'it is the same distance as the trip down. And the trail didn't seem very steep.'

Three full hours and many stops later I made it to the rim. My legs felt like tree stumps, my throat like the desert and I was wheezing like an old steam engine releasing pressure. I hadn't talked for the last hour and a half because I could only catch enough breath to put one foot in front of the other.

I was reminded of a simple principle that applies to much of life.

Going downhill is easier than going up.

It is easier to go down a slide than to climb a ladder.

It is easier to sled down a hill than to walk back up.

It seems to take a long time for a roller coaster to get up the first hill but when it starts down the ride is incredibly fast.

It is easier to gain weight that it is to lose it.

It is easier to start smoking than it is to quit.

You get the point.

Downhill is easier than uphill. It is easier to sin than to resist.

Have you ever caught a fish? I have actually stood at the end of a dock and seen fish swimming around right in front of me. When I drop my line in the water, fish come over to look at it. Some will nibble a little. Then one takes the bait and I begin to reel him in. Later on I cook and eat the fish that took the bait.

James talks about sin this way. I call it 'Fish Hook Theology' because it resembles what I just described.

> Let no one say when he is tempted, "I am being tempted by God," for God cannot be tempted with evil, and he himself tempts no one. But each person is tempted when he is lured and enticed by his own desire. Then desire when it has conceived gives

birth to sin, and sin when it is fully grown brings
forth death.
Do not be deceived, my beloved brothers.
James 1:13-16

James states a clear and unavoidable truth: When you
are tangled up with temptation don't blame God – blame
yourself.

We are tempted in the area of our sinful tendencies.
We all have them; so let's admit it. Once you know what
your tendencies are, you can strategize with the Holy Spirit
so you don't fall prey to yourself. Our tendencies are our
own. 'Each person is tempted when he is lured and enticed
by his own desire.'

'You mean I tempt myself?'

Thanks for asking! YES!

Not only do we tempt ourselves; but we have an
amazing capacity to fool ourselves at the same time. Our
sin nature when nurtured becomes a factory producing
self lies. It is difficult to embrace God's wisdom when our
conscience is distorted. We can train our conscience to live
with contradiction. Saying and doing 'spiritual' things while
grooming our favorite sin just under the surface unseen by
others.

The LORD speaking through His prophet Jeremiah
says, 'The heart is deceitful above all things and beyond
cure. Who can understand it?' He is talking about the same
thing James addresses.

I have the ability to fool myself.

'How does the devil fit into this?' Good question! His agents of evil observe our behavior and learn our weaknesses. These demonic agents help nudge us along by providing tempting scenarios that complement our individual weaknesses.

But, the devil and his crew don't always get involved. Too often, we do all the work for them.

James uses six words to describe the Fish Hook Process. Each word builds upon the previous word to form a flow of events that cause our downhill hike into sin.

Lured has to do with looking at what we desire. No action is taken but your mind and emotions are busy examining, evaluating and deciding.

Enticed is phase two. Nibbling takes place as we assure ourselves that 'just a taste' won't hurt. The problem is that it tastes good. Nibbling can go on for a while as you work at numbing your conscience to future guilt. You also need time to let your mind convince you that you can manage to continue nibbling without going any further.

Conceived happens when we take the bite that sets the hook. You've become careless in your nibbling because it is going so well. You persuade yourself that you're still in control. You impulsively take a bigger bite – the one with the hook. You are connected to the sin in a much deeper way now than you anticipated. You begin to think more strategically about keeping your sin hidden.

Birth is what happens as we are reeled in. You have set up your conscience to be manipulated into telling yourself that you are still in control. The truth is that you haven't been in control for quite a while. Now you are hooked and your sin owns you!

Fully grown refers to the development process as we mature in our sin. Your sin develops a growing root system in your life. The roots get stronger and deeper. Your skill managing your sin increases – you get good at it. Your imagination has become captivated by it. You find new avenues to explore as you go to the next level. An ongoing growth factor in this part of the process is your ability to deceive others. You are getting away with your sin. Your false conclusion is that no one, including God, is smart enough to catch you. You convince yourself that you are smart and that everyone else is stupid.

Death is the last part of the process. You become consumed or careless (usually both). Or God decides it's time to make your secret known. This seems to happen suddenly. Often you don't see it coming because you are blinded to the sin discovery process. Valuable things that you took for granted die as others find out what God already knows. You may face the death of trust in your most important relationships. You may experience the death of respect from those who gave respect to you so easily before. You will have to face the death of your integrity as you discover how broken you've become inside.

These things can be restored. But remember, the walk uphill is much more difficult and takes longer.

I generally ask people caught in sin how long the process of falling took them. I encourage them to start their timeline from the first step down. If I were standing at the rim of a canyon of temptation and I knew that the first step would eventually lead to my death; I wouldn't take it. Something inside of me broke down and I lost my ability to think with the mind of Christ. My internally warning system was faulty and I was unable to think clearly about the consequences I would face as a result of taking that first step.

There are cities and villages on the oceans that have tsunami early warning systems. The system evaluates pre-programmed factors to determine when the potential for danger exists. The alarm sounds and most people run immediately to pre-designated safety areas. There are always some people who stay on the beach in the path of the tsunami. They die because they didn't take the right action when the warning sounded. They may not take the warning seriously or think that they will be safe in a place of their own choosing.

Because we are believers, we need to make sure that our warning system is set up and maintained properly. Our warning system is the person of God's Holy Spirit working with our mind, emotions and conscience. Too often we set ourselves up for failure by not knowing how our system works. The Holy Spirit is infallible because He is God. He is also internal since He dwells within us. He is insightful because as God, He knows us better than we know ourselves.

Setting up your warning system:

Step 1 – Make sure that you have a warning system. The Holy Spirit only lives inside people who have a trust relationship with Jesus. Those who truly believe that Jesus died for their sin and rose from the dead.

Step 2 – Discipline yourself to keep your warning system up to date. Surrender your conscience to the Holy Spirit daily. If you sense Him convincing you that something is risky or downright dangerous; trust His instincts.

Step 3 – Review the manual daily. Spend time reading the Bible and thinking about it every day. The Holy Spirit inspired the authors of the Bible knowing that we need instruction for daily living.

Step 4 – Communicate, communicate, communicate! Talk to God about Himself and yourself. Practice developing an ongoing conversation with God.

When Sheila and I travel in the car she sits in the seat next to me. If a thought comes to mind, I can tell her on the spot. God is with you everywhere and always. You can tell Him anything wherever you are. He is with you!

ACTION POINTS

1. Is there a potential sin that you are nibbling at?

2. Name it to God right now.

3. Apply the 4 Step Warning System to the situation you named above. Activate it, Keep it updated and use it!

❊ ❊ ❊

FOR SMALL GROUP DISCUSSION

1. Why is it important to solve problems early?

2. What are some sins that are common in our society? List them.

3. Choose one or two sins from your list. Discuss how 'Fish Hook Theology' could happen in the life of someone who is attracted to each sin listed.

4. How would you solve the sin problems you chose using your Warning System?

A friend shared a true story with me recently that caused me to shake my head in disbelief.

A young man broke into two homes and stole some fairly valuable items. The police caught up with him and the offended parties decided to prosecute.

He displayed little remorse after his arrest but as time went by he realized the folly of his ways. He decided to plead guilty and cooperate with the police. The prosecutor put in a good word on his behalf to the judge.

The judge went easy on him. After sentencing him to prison, the judge suspended the sentence and put him on probation.

The only conditions were that he meet with a parole officer once in a while and take occasional drug tests.

Everyone in his family was relieved by the judge's decision.

The young man was so happy that he decided to celebrate. The problem is that he celebrated with drugs.

The problem came to light when he failed the drug test. You see, he chose to celebrate the night before his first drug test.

Tangled up in a mess of bad choices!

Chapter 3
Stupid comes with strings attached

He is leading the Boston Marathon by nearly a minute. He only has a mile to the finish line. He is on pace and his game plan is working perfectly. Suddenly he makes a sharp right turn. Running through the crowd and over the sidewalk, he enters an ice cream parlor. He orders two scoops of chocolate almond in a waffle cone. He then asks the server to hurry. He finishes the race walking at a pace that allows him to enjoy his ice cream. He finishes 425th.

At the post race interview our fictitious runner is asked why he stopped for ice cream. His response, 'I don't know! I just felt like I needed to.'

Why would he do something so foolish when the race was going so well? Why do we take frivolous detours when our lives are going in the right direction? Why do we sacrifice something of great importance for a short lived pleasure?

Undercurrents

Yes, undercurrents.

Those things about ourselves that lurk within. Desires we keep in check because if they came to the surface they would really mess us up. We each have our own thoughts, feelings and desires that we hold in check constantly. Each of us expends a certain amount of energy attempting to say, 'No' to desires that could captivate us if we let them loose.

We know that if we were ever to act on our suppressed desires the consequences could make us like the marathon runner. We also know that if certain circumstances were presented we would face the strongest temptations of our life.

John Edwards is a former U.S. Senator and Vice-Presidential Candidate. He has that clean cut All-American boy look. I don't know much about him personally. There is however a piece of information I do know. You probably heard it on the news – every channel, every day for two weeks!

John Edwards' wife had cancer. While she was going through the illness, he had an affair with another woman. The other woman became pregnant and had a baby.

My first reaction to this news was, "What a bad guy! How could he do that to his poor wife?"

The next time I listened to the news, with breaking new developments, God the Holy Spirit immediately reminded me that there were more people affected by Edwards' sin than his wife. There is God Himself who is offended. Edwards also sinned against his own self (1Corinthians 6:18). The news also reported that he had offended his family, friends and constituents. There was very little understanding or compassion going in John Edwards direction. What a tangled up mess!

I strongly suspect that his undercurrent surfaced. I also strongly suspect that if any one of us let our undercurrents surface we would be entangled as well.

God's Holy Spirit also reminded me that Jesus is into restoration and recovery in a big way. He died and then rose from His grave to make restoration and recovery possible for all who come to Him.

At the beginning of Hebrews Chapter 12, the writer challenges us to remember the saints mentioned in Chapter 11. Each one is an example of persevering faith. When their undercurrents surfaced, they clung to the LORD. The writer begins chapter twelve with a powerful and very difficult charge.

> Therefore, since we are surrounded by such a great cloud of witnesses, let us throw off everything that hinders and the sin that so easily entangles. And let us run with perseverance the race marked out for us, fixing our eyes on Jesus, the pioneer and perfecter of faith. For the joy set before him he endured the cross, scorning its shame, and sat down at the right hand of the throne of God. Consider him who endured such opposition from sinners, so that you will not grow weary and lose heart. Hebrews 12:1-3

Notice how easily sin ties us up.

I picture myself tangled in fishing line standing in front of a large dumpster. The line is light weight but very strong. It also tangles better than anything man has ever invented! It's wrapped around me. I am desperately attempting to untangle and untie the line from my arms when someone walks up and says, 'Need some help?'

My first instinct is to say, 'No, I can handle it.' Even though I'm thinking, 'I'll never figure this mess out!'

But, in a moment of frustration and humility, I say, 'Take your best shot. I'm pretty sure this is hopeless. Every time I think I'm making progress I realize that I'm just making it worse!'

Have you ever met one of those old guys who like to fish a lot? The man helping me is like that. He looks at the mess, picks just the right spot and begins to undo my dilemma with amazing skill.

While he is working he asks me how I got into this situation. I tell him my self-complimentary blame-free version. While he works, he says simple truths that float into my soul. I feel secure with him.

As our conversation continues I see how I really got tangled up. It begins to make sense. And it's my fault. The thing is; I *actually admit* to him that it's my fault.

He says, 'I know.'

When I finish the true version of my story, he asks, 'Are you really sorry?'

'Yes, I really am!'

'Do you want to get tangled up again?'

'No! Absolutely not!'

He has finished removing the fishing line and I am free.

He hands the tangled pile of line to me. I stare at it reflecting on my own stupidity for getting into the mess. It began so simply, yet became so complicated.

I had denied, ignored and rationalized myself into sin and it was so easy.

'Throw it in the dumpster', he holds up the lid.

I throw the tangled mess into the dumpster.

'Are you serious about avoiding the mess in the future?'

'Very serious.'

'Good, follow me!'

'OK, what's your name?'

'Jesus'

I laugh and smile, 'I knew that right after you walked up.' I'm not surprised. He was way too good with my mess to be anybody else.

'Want to see something cool? Look at the dumpster.' He smiles.

'God's Dumpster!' I read the sign on the front and laugh with a real sense of hope and joy.

'I paid for that', he says as I follow him down the road.

'I know. Thanks.'

Restoration and recovery or staying tangled up in that stupid mess. I choose R & R!

Take a lesson from Cain. Both he and his brother Abel brought offerings to the LORD. The LORD had regard for Abel and his offering but not for Cain and his offering. God was displeased with Cain's attitude in bringing the offering.

Cain became jealous and angry toward Abel. God challenged Cain with these words, 'And if you do not do well, sin is crouching at your door. Its desire is for you. But you must rule over it.'

God told Cain that he had a heart problem that was influencing his emotions. This distorted Cain's ability to understand the real problem. At this point in the conversation Cain was in a danger zone. He had two choices at this critical juncture. He could decide to back away from the danger; and ask God to help him defuse the ticking bomb in his heart. Or he could obey his feelings, walk through the door and see what happens.

When we let our emotions rule us; sin crouches at our door. When we make that really bad decision and walk through the door; sin pounces and takes control. The most influential factors for Cain had to do with satisfying his wounded pride. Right and wrong were not an issue when making his decision to walk through the door. When Cain killed his brother he had a sense of power and satisfaction.

He was sure he had a good plan. He talked his brother into walking out in a field with him. In the middle of the field, he murdered Abel. Now Cain is known all over the world as the guy who let his emotional undercurrents float to the surface and was unable to stay in control.

God gave us emotions to enrich our life experiences, not to rule our lives. He also gave us a mind to help us process and think through our decisions before we make them. He endowed us with a will that weighs and gives order to the things we are told by our mind and emotions. Don't forget the conscience. All four of these must be influenced by God to function properly. When our emotions rule the other three, we make impulsive and self gratifying decisions.

A mentor of mine once told me that when a person makes an emotional commitment to a position; often truth and common sense mean nothing to him.

I have discovered that all too often this is true.

Cain was ruled by his emotions. Sin pounced. He killed his brother.

An emotionally driven life will be a tangled mess. Blessed are the balanced!

He was the treasurer of the young floundering ministry. They never had much money but he made it work. Truth be told, he was good with money.

He liked others coming to him asking for funds. A subtle undercurrent of power and control seeped into his heart. He began to see opportunities to reward himself for his efforts. Taking some of the money didn't seem so bad. After all, he deserved it. He told himself, 'No one else can do what I do.'

After a couple of years the leader was making noises about leaving. Ministry finances would be greatly affected. So Judas began thinking about taking care of himself.

Approaching the people he thought would win in the end was smart in his mind. By now, his sin had made him stupid. He sold out, betraying Jesus for thirty pieces of silver.

Problem was that Judas didn't realize what they would do to Jesus. Trying to untangle his mess himself, he returned the money. His regret turned to unquenchable anguish and he took his own life.

Judas was a smart man. But when he let the sinful undercurrent in his life come to the surface, his sin made him stupid.

While Cain's sin issue exploded; Judas' sin slowly progressed until he was captivated.

Judas took the time to work out the details. Managing fraud became a learned skill over time. This intelligent man learned how to live a life of contradiction.

Each of us has the same negative potential.

When I consider Cain and Judas I am hit by the reality that I need to protect myself. So I give myself a strong directive:

'Self', I say with great conviction, 'Rule your emotions! Manage your thinking!'

'I will! I will for sure! I will begin now and keep these directives every day as long as I live!' I feel spiritually strong at that moment.

Giving myself directives makes me feel good for a short time. I eventually falter so I amend them or make new directives. I end up frustrated because I know that I can't rule my emotions or manage my thinking on my own.

Self control is one of the nine fruit of the Spirit listed in Galatians 5:22-23. Since it's a fruit of the Holy Spirit, He should be in charge of growing it in me. My role is to make sure the soil of my soul is conducive to growing fruit.

I have finally figured out that I don't need directives. What I need is trusting surrender. Committing to growth by submitting to the Master Gardner. Listening to what His influence says and doing it. (Not adjusting it or watering it down so I have control.)

I want to be the real me serving the real God.

I don't want to adjust who I am to look and act like the people who dictate what a believer looks, acts and talks like. I want to be me – for Christ!

I also don't want to create my own personal view of God that only includes things about Him that I like. If I did that I would eliminate wrath, condemnation, a slice of holiness and a few other things. I would end up with my own version of God; not the real one true God. If we all do this, soon we will have no idea who God really is.

I want the real God; the one who created the real me.

This is important! I have to spend time talking to Him about the undercurrents I am holding in check. I need to discipline myself to follow His wisdom and instruction about disarming those things. He may want me to confess to someone or to seek advice from a Godly person. I'll have to do that since I'm serious.

Talking to God and listening to what He says. It's the simple things that keep us from being stupid.

The fear of the LORD is the beginning of knowledge, but fools despise wisdom and instruction. Proverbs 1:7

The fear of the LORD is the beginning of wisdom, and knowledge of the Holy One is understanding. Proverbs 9:10

The fear of the LORD is the beginning of wisdom; all who follow his precepts have good understanding. To him belongs eternal praise. Psalm 111:10

Wow! God repeats Himself a lot! We had better pay attention - this is important!

ACTION POINTS

1. Are you tangled up in a sin?

2. Explain it to God. The whole mess from the beginning until right now.

3. As you tell God your story, ask for forgiveness along the way as the Holy Spirit prompts you.

4. Give your mess to Him. Ask Him to start making corrections in your thinking, feelings and will.

❋ ❋ ❋

FOR SMALL GROUP DISCUSSION

1. What are some of the things in our lives that distract or interrupt our ability to hear God clearly?

2. List the Fruit of the Spirit in Galatians 5:22-23

3. Discuss the contrast with the deeds of the flesh listed in Galatians 5:19-21.

4. How will you live out Galatians 5:24-26?

Police in Twin Falls Idaho stopped a 19 year old local man and arrested him after he gave them a fake name.

How did they know?

Dylan Contreras had his real name tattooed on his arm.

Police took him into custody on outstanding warrants, including one for providing false information.

He tried to hide the obvious!

Did he think they wouldn't notice?

World Magazine

Chapter 4
You can't keep secrets from God!

'Everyone tells someone! And when they do they always enhance the original version.'

I don't remember who told me that in my early years of ministry. He turned out to be right about most people.

Have you ever trusted someone by sharing a personal issue in your life? A week or a month later you hear a distorted version of your issue from someone else. It bothers you that your trusted friend broke your confidence.

But, you don't stop to consider that you have done this too.

Let's relive the conversation:

'You are the only person I'm sharing this with. Make sure you tell no one else.'

'Thanks for trusting me. I will never speak of this to anyone. This is our secret. I promise.'

The hearer later becomes the teller.

'I would like to ask you to pray for Kevin. He's has an issue in his life that he is struggling with.'

'Tell me more so I can pray intelligently.'

'I'm only telling you this because I trust you. And I know Kevin would trust you too.'

'Does he know you are talking to me about his issue?'

'Oh no, and you have to promise not to tell him. He told me in confidence and I'm telling you in confidence.'

'Thanks for trusting me. I will never speak of this to anyone. This is our secret. I promise.'

Hearer number two then becomes the teller, repeating the same conversation with hearer number three who is soon to become the teller, telling someone else and so on and so on……

Someone other than the original hearer asks you one day how you are doing with your 'issue'. You ask the person, 'Who told you about this?' He names teller number eight.

You ask him what exactly he knows. He tells you a version significantly more serious than the original.

You wonder if you can trust anyone. *Is any secret safe?*

Congressman Anthony Weiner never had a chance.

He used his cell phone to tweet lewd pictures to a woman who was not his wife. This is a stupid thing to do even with your wife! (Hebrews 13:4)

The woman shared the photos with someone else. A reporter got involved. The reporter got a news network involved and the Congressman's sin became ring one in that week's media circus.

He lied and denied. A couple of days later he confessed. He held a press conference and became another example that sin makes you stupid. Other women came forward and the ripples from his secret sin turned into a tsunami sized personal scandal.

Some fellow members of congress called for his resignation. He acted on their pressure and stepped down.

But that wasn't his biggest problem. His wife of one year was pregnant. He had to try and save his marriage.

Most Americans didn't know who Anthony Weiner was before his sin catapulted him into the national news spotlight.

Jesus talked about this negative spotlight:

> Meanwhile, when a crowd of many thousands had gathered, so that they were trampling on one another, Jesus began to speak first to his disciples, saying: "Be on your guard against the yeast of the Pharisees, which is hypocrisy. There is nothing concealed that will not be disclosed, or hidden that will not be made known. What you have said in the dark

will be heard in the daylight, and what you have whispered in the ear in the inner rooms will be proclaimed from the roofs. Luke 12:1-3

Wow! Talk about total disclosure!

Jesus warns His disciples about the 'leaven of the Pharisees'. Leaven by nature spreads throughout the bread dough until it reaches every part. He is talking about hypocrisy. Acting like someone you are not so you *look* spiritual without *being* spiritual. Hypocrisy is all about appearance. And it is contagious!

> Your boasting is not good. Do you not know that a little leaven leavens the whole lump? Cleanse out the old leaven that you may be a new lump, as you really are unleavened. For Christ, our Passover lamb, has been sacrificed. 1 Corinthians 5:6-7

Jesus' charge to His disciples is the same as the Apostle Paul's charge to the Corinthians. We are to cleanse our lives of hypocrisy and be real. We can be real because of Jesus' personal sacrifice. His death for our sins was as real as it gets! He knows us deeply and loves us greatly.

Our unrealness will be shouted from the rooftops when Jesus comes to judge.

Be smart and get real now!

I wonder if the Congressman will get real with Jesus. I hope he experiences the brokenness of a sorrowful sinner. I also hope he experiences the joy of forgiveness and new life in Jesus. It won't happen unless he practices total disclosure with our Savior.

Jesus knows everything already; but it's cleansing for us to talk to Him about it. There's something supernatural that happens to us when we ask for forgiveness. The weight of secret guilt and fear of discovery are lifted from your soul by God Himself.

You could say about Congressman Anthony Weiner: 'He is only sorry because he got caught.'

Good point! That's a great starting place!

Could God have arranged that to bring him to his knees? When the weight of sin pushes us down we realize our helplessness. Realization is a big step toward repentance which is a big step toward restoration which is a big step toward recovery .....'

Wouldn't it be smarter to confess before we get caught? Yes! How many people do you know who have done that?

Not many.

Why is that?

Sin makes you stupid!

Annanias and Sapphira witnessed a truly unselfish act of generosity. Tragically, they didn't interpret the results properly because their thinking was self-centered. Joseph, a constant encourager, sold a piece of land and gave the entire amount of the sale to the ministry. He was also called Barnabas by the apostles. His new name meant 'son of encouragement'.

Annanias and Sapphira probably thought that he received the honor of a name change because of the money he gave. They also sold a piece of property and decided to give some of the money to the ministry. There was nothing wrong with that. Until they pretended that they gave it all.

Annanias made his move in front of the whole church and laid the money at the apostle's feet. Imagine his surprise when instead of thanking him, Peter said,

> "Ananias, how is it that Satan has so filled your heart that you have lied to the Holy Spirit and have kept for yourself some of the money you received for the land? Didn't it belong to you before it was sold? And after it was sold, wasn't the money at your disposal? What made you think of doing such a thing? You have not lied just to human beings but to God."

Read the rest of the story:

> When Ananias heard this, he fell down and died. And great fear seized all who heard what had happened. Then some young men came forward, wrapped up his body, and carried him out and buried him.

> About three hours later his wife came in, not knowing what had happened. Peter asked her, "Tell me, is this the price you and Ananias got for the land?"

> "Yes," she said, "that is the price."

> Peter said to her, "How could you conspire to test the Spirit of the Lord? Listen! The feet of the men

who buried your husband are at the door, and they will carry you out also."

At that moment she fell down at his feet and died. Then the young men came in and, finding her dead, carried her out and buried her beside her husband. Great fear seized the whole church and all who heard about these events.

Annanais and Sapphira made a deadly error in their thinking. They didn't consider the God Factor. With God there are no secrets!

People can be fooled! God can't!

The secret undercurrents of our lives are not secret to God. He knows the internal battles we fight. He also knows when we are surrendered to the Holy Spirit's influence.

The **scary part** of the 'no secrets from God' truth is that He knows all the stuff about me that I don't want anyone to know. I don't want my Holy God to see my dirt. But He does.

The **refreshing part** of the 'no secrets from God' truth is that He resides in me to nurture His fruit in my soul. He can monitor our growth and struggles. He is constantly available to help us!

He not only sees my dirt; His Son died to clean me up!

I have a friend with a heart problem. The doctor injected a dye into his system and took pictures of his heart. The pictures revealed three blockages. Any one of the blockages could have caused a major heart attack! The doctor put a stent in each artery to open up the blood flow. He also put my friend on a strict diet. I think it was called the 'If it tastes good spit it out!' diet.

My friend was very disciplined in his eating habits for the first six months. One day, I caught him eating at a fast food restaurant. I chose not to order and instead I walked over and sat down to talk with him.

'Do you know what you're eating?'

'Yeah! And it tastes great!'

'Do you remember what your doctor said'

'Yeah! But this tastes great!'

'I know you feel good but you have to be careful not to drift back into your old eating habits.'

'This is the last time I'll eat here.'

'So there have been other times?'

'Well ….'

Just then another friend walked in and said, 'Hi Dennis! Seems like we see each other here every day!'

Busted!!

I then asked him the killer question, 'Does your doctor know you're here?'

He almost choked on his burger, 'Nope!'

I'm sure he didn't enjoy the rest of his lunch.

God knows when our spiritual diet is out of balance.

He knows because He's omniscient.

He also knows because when we sneak into sinful secrets we stop talking to him.

Who wants to take advice from someone who always speaks the truth? When we get caught up in secret sins; we like to revise truth so it's easier to live with ourselves. If we talk to God – it's too convicting! He never revises the truth – and truth doesn't change to accommodate our desires.

Did I mention that God is always right?

When I want to do wrong, I don't want to talk to the One who is always right. He'll tell me to stop wrong and get right!

Sometimes I just don't want to hear it! So I convince myself that if I don't tell Him; He won't know.

Sound ridiculous? It is! But remember sin makes you stupid!

ACTION POINTS

1. Write down one of your secret sins.

2. Pray. Talk to God about your sin remembering that He knows.

3. Ask Him to help you stop lying to yourself about your sin.

4. Ask for forgiveness and the strength to recognize your sinful thoughts as sin when they come to your mind.

❋ ❋ ❋

SMALL GROUP DISCUSSION

1. What do you think Peter meant when he accused Annanias and Sapphira of lying to the Holy Spirit?

2. Why do you think we try so hard to pretend we're good when we have destructive hidden sins in our lives?

A couple with a serious financial problem came to discuss their situation with their pastor.

'I just lost my job and can't make my house payment.' Jonah explained.

Pastor asked, 'Is your house the only debt you have?'

Jonah responded too quickly, 'We have a few others.'

Sue interjected, 'No, we have a ton of other payments!'

'Let's make a list of everything you owe.' Pastor took out a sheet of paper and wrote 'Everything we owe' at the top.

Suddenly there was an uncomfortable chill in the air.

'I'm not sure that's necessary!' she said while he nodded in agreement.

'Since you have no job don't you think it would be good to evaluate where you are financially?' Pastor persisted.

'Yeah, I guess so.' Jonah sounded trapped.

As the list was made the couple became visibly upset.

Their credit card debt was well over $20,000.

They owed $7,000 on their boat and $9,000 on their vacation trailer. The combined debt on their two cars was close $60,000.

They had purchased furniture two years ago on one of those 'no interest for 24 months' deals. They paid the minimum payment and were now getting slammed with a huge interest payment on what they still owed.

'How could we have been so stupid?' Jonah shouted at himself.

Over a period of time and with an accountability partner they cleaned up their financial mess. They lost their house, boat, a car and their trailer in the process. They made a deal with the credit card company for a reduced rate and payment schedule.

They downsized their lifestyle to fit their income. Then Jonah got a new job.

They immediately began buying more stuff. Big stuff – like a brand new fully loaded car. Actually, it was a truck with the capacity to haul their new travel trailer.

The pastor called on them to caution them about their finances.

When he asked, 'Why are you diving back into the same pattern that got you in trouble before?'

Their response was:

'We've learned a lot. And it won't happen again. We're smarter now.'

The pastor's response, 'Really? You can make the same mistakes on the same scale as before and get a different result?'

'Absolutely!"

'By the way,' pastor inquired, 'do you give to God's work?'

'We've always wanted to but could never quite afford it.'

Hmmmmm .... Their priorities are really mixed up!

Chapter 5

It is Stupid to Ignore History!

There were mice in my garage. I noticed when I took the garbage out one night. I decided to go hunting. I armed myself with six mouse traps, some peanut butter and cheese. I figured if they didn't like peanut butter, the cheese would be hard to resist.

As I set the traps, I came up with an idea. Why not put two traps side by side? Mice like to run along walls so this would double the temptation to walk into the trap.

While checking the traps the next morning, I discovered something that surprised me. I caught two mice! One in each of the traps that were side by side.

I considered how this may have happened. I can understand one mouse creeping up and sniffing the cheese. I could grasp that he would take a bite and the trap would snap – game over for him!

But the second mouse was perplexing. He had seen the dead mouse in the first trap. He had seen the cheese in his mouth. I would think at that point that he would get that it was dangerous and avoid making the same deadly mistake.

But he didn't!

Recent mouse history said that if the trap killed one mouse, another trap right next to it with the same bait would kill the second mouse. With recent history staring him in the face, he went for the cheese and died.

It is stupid to ignore history!

King Nebuchadnezzar was the great king of Babylon. He had expanded his empire and influence over much of the known world. In the process he conquered Judah and brought a young man named Daniel into his court. Daniel was given a special gift from God. He was able to interpret dreams and solve difficult problems. Over many years he had helped the king often with difficult problems and dreams that none of the other wise men of Babylon could handle.

After years of successful problem solving (100%); Nebuchadnezzar had an alarming dream. He called Daniel to interpret. The dream spoke of a strong judgment from God that was going to come down on the king.

Daniel told the king,

> "This is the interpretation, Your Majesty, and this is the decree the Most High has issued against my lord the king: You will be driven away from people and will live with the wild animals; you will eat grass like the ox and be drenched with the dew of heaven. Seven times will pass by for you until you acknowledge that the Most High is sovereign over all kingdoms on earth and gives them to anyone

he wishes. The command to leave the stump of the tree with its roots means that your kingdom will be restored to you when you acknowledge that Heaven rules. Therefore, Your Majesty, be pleased to accept my advice: Renounce your sins by doing what is right, and your wickedness by being kind to the oppressed. It may be that then your prosperity will continue."

Wow! Bad news for the king!

Daniel challenged the king to repent and serve God. King Nebuchadnezzar ignored the warning and went on with his life. Did he think that God was not powerful enough to do what He said He would do?

Three months went by and nothing happened. Six months went by, then nine with no judgment from God.

At the one year point the king was on the roof of his palace having an ego fest. He was impressed with his own power, intellect and glory. Suddenly, God brought the judgment! Seven years of living like an animal began.

Nebuchadnezzar ignored his history with Daniel. He had acknowledged often that Daniel spoke for God. And yet, he was in denial as to Who had authority over him.

Was he confused? Was the message from God too difficult to understand? No!

Was he in denial? Did he think he was untouchable? Yes!

His sin of arrogance caused him to turn stupid!

He learned the hard way. After seven years of living like an animal, he finally trusted God as the Almighty authority. King Nebuchadnezzar actually wrote Daniel Chapter 4. Not a very flattering account of himself. The chapter is a testimony to his step up from arrogance to humility. When you take the step from pride to humility; God will lift you up.

But that's not all.

King Nebuchadnezzar had a son named Belshazzar who became king when his father died. He liked to party. Babylon was under siege by the Medes and Persians. So Belshazzar threw a party. He ordered the sacred vessels that had been used in God's temple before Jerusalem was conquered to be brought out. He and his nobles desecrated the vessels by drinking from them and mocking God.

Suddenly a hand appeared and wrote on the wall. The king was alarmed. His legs began to shake with fear. He became pale. His own wise men couldn't decipher the writing on the wall.

The queen suggested they bring in Daniel. She knew all about his history with King Nebuchadnezzar.

Belshazzar not only brought Daniel in, he offered him the third highest position in the kingdom if he could interpret the handwriting on the wall. Daniel had a great opportunity for advancement. He refused the promotion!

Daniel knew history. So did Belshazzar but he ignored it. So Daniel gave him a lesson from King Nebuchadnezzar's life. He reminds Belshazzar that God brought his father down because of his pride. Daniel challenged Belshazzar with the humbling lesson his father learned from God.

> "But you, Belshazzar, his son, have not humbled yourself, though you knew all this. Instead, you have set yourself up against the Lord of heaven. You had the goblets from his temple brought to you, and you and your nobles, your wives and your concubines drank wine from them. You praised the gods of silver and gold, of bronze, iron, wood and stone, which cannot see or hear or understand. But you did not honor the God who holds in his hand your life and all your ways. Therefore he sent the hand that wrote the inscription.' Daniel 5:22-24

Belshazzar was about to be judged by God for being careless with the kingdom entrusted to his care.

"This is the inscription that was written:

MENE, MENE, TEKEL, PARSIN

"Here is what these words mean:

Mene: God has numbered the days of your reign and brought it to an end.

Tekel: You have been weighed on the scales and found wanting.

Peres: Your kingdom is divided and given to the Medes and Persians." Daniel 5: 25-28

This was really bad news for Belshazzar. He was about to lose everything. God used the word 'Mene' twice to emphasize the finality of His judgment on Belshazzar. This was one of those defining moments where he needed to be smart. But Belshazzar chose to go with stupid.

> Then at Belshazzar's command, Daniel was clothed in purple, a gold chain was placed around his neck, and he was proclaimed the third highest ruler in the kingdom. :29

He acted like there was no threat. He honored Daniel with the very things that Daniel had just turned down. He didn't get the severity of the situation. His goal seemed to be for the party to continue. It didn't last long.

> That very night Belshazzar, king of the Babylonians, was slain, and Darius the Mede took over the kingdom, at the age of sixty-two.

Belshazzar's sin predisposed him to ignore God's warning through His prophet Daniel.

It is stupid to ignore history.

Dodging the consequences of sin doesn't work. History repeats itself over and over again.

We apply the 'I can dodge the consequences' theory at our convenience. When we don't get in trouble right away we assume that we never will. Remember, God let Nebuchadnezzar go for a year before His judgment came down.

The doctor had run all the tests. He was certain that his patient had cancer. The doctor reviewed what he would tell his patient. He wanted to be able to answer all the basic questions.

What kind is it and where is it?

How far has it progressed?

Is it treatable?

What treatments work best?

The doctor speaks to his patient based on his knowledge of history. He knows the historical path this particular type of cancer usually takes. He knows treatment options and success rates. Even if a treatment is new, the doctor knows the test history.

The doctor doesn't assume that his patient will beat the consequences revealed by history.

A smart patient makes treatment decisions based on the historical record.

It's about knowing history!

I was teaching a class at the Barry County jail some years ago. The class was called, 'The Truth about Consequences'. My hope was that the inmates would learn how to think about all the possible consequences and decide not to commit their next crime. After class one day, an inmate came to me and told me that he was only taking the class so he would have a certificate to show the judge in hopes of an earlier release date.

He informed me that his cellmate was teaching him all he needed to know to beat the system. He told me that his cellmate had practical experience as this was his second time in jail.

I tried to explain to him that taking advice from someone who had been incarcerated twice was ridiculous.

I have never forgotten his final words.

'We agree to disagree!'

Ignoring history sets you up for stupid.

Adam and Eve sinned in the Garden of Eden. They were judged and lost their access to that wonderful place. It's history.

Noah and seven of his family members were delivered from a worldwide flood by the hand of God. Everyone else died because of their sin. It's history.

Jesus bore the sins of all people upon Himself on the cross. He suffered a hideous death because of our sins. It's history.

Jesus rose from the dead. His sacrifice on the cross was satisfactory to God. Our future exposure to His condemning judgment is averted. It's history.

Get history right. If you don't; the consequences are serious. 'The wages of sin is death, but the free gift of God through Jesus Christ our Lord is eternal life.' Romans 6:23

So far we have learned five life-changing truths:

1. Sin turns smart people stupid!

2. The path to stupid goes downhill.

3. Stupid comes with strings attached.

4. You can't keep secrets from God.

5. It is stupid to ignore history

ACTION POINTS

1. What events/habits in your personal history do you need to give to God?

2. Take a moment to pray thanking God for Jesus and the salvation He provides for you.

3. If you are not a believer yet – think about taking this moment to invite Jesus into your life. Trust that His payment for your sins is thorough and complete. Ask Him for forgiveness and surrender you life to His masterful leadership.

❊ ❊ ❊

FOR SMALL GROUP DISCUSSION

1. Make a short personal comment about each of the five life changing truths listed on the previous page.

2. Why is it so difficult see the downhill path when you're on it?

3. Name some sin issues and talk about the strings attached to them. Think about the collateral damage that ripples out to other people in your life.

Sin Makes You Stupid
Part 2

The More You Sin; The Stupider You Get!

Brian Sickles robbed the local Subway restaurant in Washington Pennsylvania.

But he didn't leave with any money.

Brian broke the glass door but couldn't get the money out of the cash register.

Rather than go home empty handed; he stole nine bags of potato chips.

Police followed the trail of potato chip bags and some blood from his cut hand (glass door did it!) and arrested him.

He couldn't leave empty handed! He had to take something!

I guess they didn't have any cookies out!

World Magazine

Chapter 1
The Multiplication of Stupid

She sat across from my desk in tears. Her husband was cheating on her with someone from work. I gently asked her for some background information.

'Please, tell me how you met your husband.'

'We met at a bar. He bought me a drink and we just started talking.'

'What did you talk about?'

'Our marriages mostly. We had a lot in common. Both of us were unhappy with our spouses and thinking of leaving them.'

'So you were both married to other people when you met each other?'

'Yes, and we felt guilty about that at first. But our marital problems were so much alike ... we had so much to talk about. Suddenly, one evening we realized we were in love with each other.'

'What made you decide to divorce your spouses and get married?'

'We were really seeking God's will for our future. We knew that God wanted us to get married when I got pregnant. The message was so clear. We were looking for a sign.'

'Let's review,' I said, 'Your relationship began when you cheated on your spouses. You then tried to convince yourselves that your sin was OK so you spiritualized it by praying together. Somehow out of your sin, you thought God blessed your immoral union. Am I getting it right?

'You being a little insensitive.'

'OK,' I said seeking to understand the situation, 'let me restate the whole thing. John was cheating on his wife with you. He divorced his wife to marry you. Now you are surprised that he is cheating on you with someone else.'

'Exactly'

'So you are really innocent in all this?'

'Yes'

'I'm going to tell you something that you never want to forget. Are you ready?'

'Yes'

'Sin makes you stupid'

'That doesn't make sense at all.'

'You sinned when you met John. You continued to sin with John. Now someone else is doing the same thing with John that you did when you met him. Is John sinning?'

'Absolutely!'

'Is John being stupid?'

'Very stupid!'

'Do you think John's first wife thought you were stupid?'

'I don't get what you're saying.'

'I know.'

The more you sin the stupider you get.

God gave each of us a conscience to witness what goes on in the inner workings of our being. A conscience in good working condition filters our thoughts, feelings and actions accusing or defending them. If your conscience functions properly your life will be in unison with God's will. The Bible calls this a good conscience. When God the Holy Spirit checks out your conscience He lets you know when and how you are at fault. When God sees your conscience as blameless you are positioned to make quality, God honoring choices in life.

But there is a callous that develops around your inner self when you sin continually. Your conscience becomes distorted and unable to function properly. The Bible calls this a defiled conscience. I think about it as polluted. When we go through the process of getting used to our sin, we dump bad thoughts and feelings into our clear conscience so it becomes clouded with the pollution of sin.

How does this happen?

The infatuation with sin becomes greater than the guilt we experience.

Whatever 'reason' we make up to justify our pet sin is a lie. The bottom line is that we love the sin enough to hurt ourselves and others to have it.

Remember your dating days? Boy meets girl; they flirt; they go out. Both are on their best behavior. They want to impress each other. They succeed and the infatuation process begins. They are in 'love' but don't really know each other. She hasn't seen him disrespect his mom. He hasn't seen her manipulate her friends.

Early in the relationship when negative things happen they are excused because the newness of the relationship feels so good. Some months later the infatuation is gone and she complains that he takes her for granted. He thinks she's trying to control him. They try to break up a few times but always get back together. They eventually agree that they can't live without each other –so they get married.

Sound familiar? That's how sin works on us. We meet sin; we flirt with it; we start a relationship.

Changing the way we think about sin is difficult because we love it. We don't like to think something we love is bad.

Our relationship with sin develops in four progressive stages.

Stage One:

Input occurs when we seek to know about something that may please us. We pursue thinking about it. Letting it run around in our imagination. Taking a test drive with it to see how the sin performs. After all, we have to decide if it's worth going after.

Stage Two:

Unbalance happens when we deal with the guilt attached to a sin we enjoy. It becomes a 'guilty pleasure'.

Stage Three:

Adaptation follows as we manipulate our con-science, our mind and our emotions to reduce guilt. We actually end up suppressing our guilt because it can't be removed. We teach ourselves to work around it and in spite of it. This is difficult because the parts of our lives that are 'good' are negatively affected by the part that is 'bad'. We convince ourselves that the problem is not the sin but the guilt that is attached to the sin. In our 'sin makes you stupid' stupor, we actually believe that getting rid of the guilt will make everything OK. So we put it in a compartment inside ourselves and lock the door. Whenever we open the door, even slightly, we experience the painful twangs as if we just started our sin yesterday.

Some of us attempt to hold our guilt down like a giant spring hoping that it will weaken over time. One of the reasons many people are thankful when they get caught is because they are tired of holding down the spring. When they confess, the pressure is released and they have a sense of relief.

Stage Four:

Control comes as we become mature in the sin. The relationship shifts over time. Like the dating couple, you try to break up. You keep going back and soon feel trapped by the sin. You don't think you can live without it so you 'marry' your sin. It becomes an important part of your life. You know this because you begin organizing other important things in your life around your sin. It owns you!

King David was the greatest king in Israel's history. He was a great leader and warrior. He was known as 'a man after God's own heart'. It seemed strange that he sent his army against the Ammonites without him. Something was wrong inside David's heart. Read how things played out for him.

> One evening David got up from his bed and walked around on the roof of the palace. From the roof he saw a woman bathing. The woman was very beautiful, and David sent someone to find out about her. The man said, "She is Bathsheba, the daughter of Eliam and the wife of Uriah the Hittite." Then David sent messengers to get her. She came to him, and he slept with her. (Now she was purifying herself from her monthly uncleanness.) Then she went back home. The woman conceived and sent word to David, saying, "I am pregnant." 2 Samuel 11:2-5

Input: King David stayed home. What was he thinking about? Perhaps he had a secret desire for the woman who lived next door. He saw her bathing from the roof of his palace late at night. Did he know she would be there? Had he looked before? Did he see her 'accidently on purpose'? Or was he surprised to see her bathing but decided to watch for a while anyway.

Unbalance: David sent someone to find out about the woman. His people told him that she was married to Uriah. Uriah was a soldier at war serving in King David's army. He had to filter that information through his conscience and decide to either discard the lust he was experiencing or act upon it. He sent for her. They committed adultery. She went home. She came back a while later and told him she was pregnant.

Adaptation: David didn't want it to be known that he was an adulterer. What would the people think if they knew their king had a moral problem? David needed to do damage control. He needed to adapt. He brought Uriah home from the war hoping that he would have relations with Bathsheba and think the pregnancy was his doing. Uriah, a man of honor, refused to sleep with his wife while his men were at war. David got him drunk hoping he would lower his standards. He didn't. David sent a confidential note with Uriah when he went back to the front. The note, for Uriah's commander, contained a plot to place Uriah before the enemy in such a way that he would not survive. David adapted by getting rid of a major obstacle to his relationship with Bathsheba – her husband!

Control: Uriah died (many other soldiers died in the process of setting him up). David used the opportunity to marry Bathsheba. The pregnancy appeared to be part of their marriage. The sin had multiplied.

David had added a great deal to his first sin.

Stupid multiplies!

David committed adultery.

To cover up the adulterous activity, David committed deceit.

His deceit had layers of depth:

(1) Attempted to deceive Uriah into sleeping with Bathsheba.

(2) Got Uriah drunk hoping he would sleep with Bathsheba

(3) Sent a note carried by Uriah ordering his death.

(4) His army had a different battle plan to insure Uriah's death. In the process many good men were also killed. Deceived into believing in the plan.

(5) The messenger carrying news of the defeat was instructed to inform the king in a 'by the way' fashion that Uriah had been killed in battle.

Sin upon sin upon sin and on it goes!

When we are at risk of being found out, we try to manage the fallout. The problem is that we create more damage.

David committed the sin of adultery. By managing the fallout he committed at least five other sins.

King David was a good man. Smart enough to run an entire kingdom. But he slipped into stupid and it multiplied.

'If we claim to be without sin, we deceive ourselves and the truth is not in us. If we confess our sins, he is faithful and just and will forgive us our sins and purify us from all unrighteousness. If we claim we have not sinned, we make him out to be a liar and his word is not in us.' 1 John 1:8-10

Sin multiplies when we embrace the prideful practice of self deceit. We lose our grip on truth. When you lose your grip on truth you will call God a liar in your heart. Uncertainty will rule your life because you trust yourself over God. Your sin has made you untrustworthy.

Why not take the route of certainty? Confess! Jesus will always forgive the sincere confession. He is so amazing! He not only forgives us but cleans us up.

Confession is a no brainer even if you are caught up in a mess of multiplied sin.

He died so we could be forgiven. He's serious about us! Take Him up on it!

ACTION POINTS

1. Memorize 1 John 1:8-10.

2. Read about David's sin in 2 Samuel Chapter 11.

3. Read about the Prophet Nathan confronting David in 2 Samuel Chapter 12.

How did David move from denial to confession?

4. Write your personalized version of Psalm 51:17.

❋ ❋ ❋

FOR SMALL GROUP DISCUSSION

1. Read David's prayer of confession in Psalm 51
List the things David requested of God.

What does David say that shows you that he took ownership of his sin?

2. Share your personalized version of verse 17.

3. For you personally, what is the most difficult part of taking ownership of your sin?

We took our Wisconsin youth group to Michigan for summer camp. While we were there my wife took a SMALL group of kids to Kmart. Rick, an eighteen year old senior, packed his pockets with items from the shelves. He had CD's and candy mostly.

As the group was leaving the store a security guard approached Rick and escorted him into the manager's office. My wife went along and was shocked to see the amount of stuff Rick had stolen.

The police were called. Because Rick was eighteen, he could be prosecuted as an adult and placed in the county jail.

My wife somehow talked the manager and the police into letting Rick go. She assured them that his parents would deal with him appropriately.

As they were leaving the store, my wife asked Rick if he had anything else in his pockets. He laughed and said 'yes'.

She returned to the manager's office with him and made him return the rest of the loot.

They still released him. The last we heard, Rick's adult life was a mess.

Stupidity combined with pride makes you a prime target for the evil one.

Chapter 2
Dare to be Stupid!

Nimrod was captivated by pride. His natural abilities to hunt and fight gave him a reputation that confirmed his prideful attitude. Genesis 10 lists the family tree of Noah's sons. The list is just a list until you get to Nimrod.

> 'Cush was the father of Nimrod, who became a mighty warrior on the earth. He was a mighty hunter before the LORD; that is why it is said, "Like Nimrod, a mighty hunter before the LORD." The first centers of his kingdom were Babylon, Uruk, Akkad and Kalneh, in Shinar. From that land he went to Assyria, where he built Nineveh, Rehoboth Ir, Calah and Resen, which is between Nineveh and Calah—which is the great city.

Nimrod is remembered as a mighty warrior and hunter. The word 'mighty' is used three times to describe him. He 'became a mighty hunter on the earth'. The reference to being a hunter also refers to his abilities as a warrior. His goal was to become the best of the best – and he did it!

"He was a mighty hunter before the LORD; that is why it is said, 'Like Nimrod, a mighty hunter before the LORD.'"

Remember Michael Jordan The great basketball player with the Chicago Bulls? Kids would say, 'I want to be like Mike!' A Gatorade commercial shows short clips of

Jordan in game situations making amazing moves and scoring baskets. The song promotes that if you drink Gatorade you can be like Mike.

Back in the day, kids said, 'I want to be like Nimrod!' He was a superstar in his time. His mightiness was legend. And he wanted more! The short phrase 'before the LORD' tells us that he put himself first ahead of the LORD. The strong implication is that he shook his fist at God and determined to build his own world his way.

Most people followed him instead of God!

Their mission statement was simple and directive; 'Come let us build ourselves a city, with a tower that reaches to the heavens, so that we may make a name for ourselves and not be scattered over the face of the whole earth.' (Genesis 11:4).

Their purpose was to be like Nimrod!

When we are caught up in the emotional state that accompanies the sin of pride; we lose our ability to grasp the big picture of God's abilities.

Tim showed up with just a hammer in his tool belt. Granted, it was a big roughing hammer. We were putting the walls in our new church gym. He grabbed a fistful of nails and went to work. He drove each nail with one swift hit. He was amazing with that hammer! But that was the only tool he had – or so I thought. After a while he went to his truck and came back with two different types of power saws to help the cutting crew keep up with him. He had other tools too. A tape measure and a carpenters square among others.

Each tool had a purpose and was used when the situation arose.

People in the days of Nimrod remembered the flood judgment of God during his great grandfather Noah's time. Under Nimrod's leadership the people decided that God had only two tools with which to exercise His judgment – fire and water. He had already used water and promised He wouldn't flood the earth again. So fire was the only tool he had left – or so they thought.

Genesis 11 records the folly of their thinking. With Nimrod as their leader the people decided to build their own city and make up their own worship system. The problem was that God told them to spread out, multiply and fill the earth. Like many of us, they didn't want to leave each other and be stretched by obedience to God. So, they decided to stay together and design a series of new gods. After all, who would want only one God when you can have many to choose from? Then, if you didn't like a particular god you could simply choose another; giving you a sense of control over the god or gods you chose.

Historians tell us that the first Babylonians designed a variety of gods from which to choose. We tend to like this concept too. We worship money for what it gives us. Power for what we can take with it. Success for the feeding of our egos. We can have all three of these as our gods and add comfort or whatever else we want to our god list. We do fine with this as long as we have control and things outside our grasp cooperate. When our self made gods begin to crumble; we turn to the one true God and blame Him!

The original Babylonians knew two things for sure. They knew that God would deal with them because of their sin. They also knew that He wouldn't use a flood to bring His judgment upon them.

These original Babylonians made the assumption that God would use fire to judge them. That is why they built the city and worship tower out of fire proof brick and used tar instead of mortar.

Nimrod was so confident that he convinced himself that he could out think God.

In his prideful state he was sure that he and his people were judgment proof!

Imagine their surprise when God used a different tool to judge them and accomplish His will! He confused their languages, making it difficult for them to communicate with each other. This also created linguistic groups of people. Those who could understand each other went off together.

The city and tower were not finished. The city was called Babel because that's what people did when the LORD confused their language.

Nimrod continued to shake his fist at God. He built other cities in the area of Babel. He had strong sinful determination to act as his own authority. He tried to stay on the plains of Shinar. He eventually left the area and built five other cities. Two of these are among the greatest empires the world has known. Both Babylon and Assyria (Nineveh was the capital) conquered Israel.

Nimrod was a great leader. Sadly he used his abilities against God rather than for Him. Nimrod was a very intelligent leader. He knew how to think strategically and convince others to follow him. He convinced the whole world to follow him and disobey God! We cannot disregard his influence and abilities. His legacy will continue throughout history until the fall of Babylon and the judgment of the Antichrist at the return of Jesus.

What went wrong with Nimrod?
Great talent
Great communicator
Great warrior
Great leader
Great ambition
Great arrogance

Paul addresses Nimrod's philosophy of life in his letter to the Roman believers. In the first chapter of his letter he writes:

> For although they knew God, they neither glorified him as God nor gave thanks to him, but their thinking became futile and their foolish hearts were darkened. Although they claimed to be wise, they became fools and exchanged the glory of the immortal God for images made to look like a mortal human being and birds and animals and reptiles.

> Therefore God gave them over in the sinful desires of their hearts to sexual impurity for the degrading of their bodies with one another. They exchanged the truth about God for a lie, and worshiped and served created things rather than the Creator— who is forever praised. Amen.

Because of this, God gave them over to shameful lusts. Even their women exchanged natural sexual relations for unnatural ones. In the same way the men also abandoned natural relations with women and were inflamed with lust for one another. Men committed shameful acts with other men, and received in themselves the due penalty for their error.

Furthermore, just as they did not think it worthwhile to retain the knowledge of God, so God gave them over to a depraved mind, so that they do what ought not to be done. They have become filled with every kind of wickedness, evil, greed and depravity. They are full of envy, murder, strife, deceit and malice. They are gossips, slanderers, God-haters, insolent, arrogant and boastful; they invent ways of doing evil; they disobey their parents; they have no understanding, no fidelity, no love, no mercy. Although they know God's righteous decree that those who do such things deserve death, they not only continue to do these very things but also approve of those who practice them.

Romans 1:21-32

There is a clear choice involved in the lives of those who reject God. The choices we make have outcomes. Nimrod's desired outcome was to set himself up as his own life authority.

Read the passage above and answer the questions below to see the actual outcome of Nimrod's philosophy of arrogance.

*What happened to their ability to think clearly? :21

*What did they claim to be? What were they really? :22

*When God gave them over to their sinful desires what was the outcome? :24/26/27/29

*Did they turn to God when they saw the outcome of their sin? :32

I heard a story recently about two burglars. They broke into the home of an elderly woman and robbed her. One of them was caught and the other is still at large. The one that was caught refuses to name his partner. His position is that it is not honorable to rat out your fellow thief. What's wrong with his thinking?

He is basically saying that it is honorable to rob an elderly woman.

It is honorable to break into someone else's home and take their stuff.

But it is not honorable to turn in the other burglar who will continue his 'honorable' line of work by breaking into the homes of the elderly.

The burglar claims to have honor but he is not honorable. His sin has clouded his ability to think in an honorable fashion. He has a built in desire to be honorable because he was created in God's image. At some point in his life he decided to exchange the truth of God for a lie about who he really is. He wants the appearance of honor without the substance.

The burglar should be thinking about what he did to mess up his life. Paul gives us an ongoing list of the negative attitudes and actions of those who want to 'be like Nimrod'.

*Don't give God credit for being God (:21)

*Don't be thankful to God (:21)

*Exchange God's place with lesser things (:23)

*Trade the truth about who God is for lies about Him.

*Transfer the worship He deserves to things you have created yourself. (:25)

*Consider it a waste of your time to think about God, His ways and His will. (:28)

The issue here is not about designer idols or building cities and towers. The issue is about the hearts of those who were motivated to act against God. The motivation comes before the action happens. The motivational catalyst with Nimrod and the Babylonians was pride.

Babylon still rules in the hearts of many. The Babylonian view of life is thriving in our world today. The problem with pride is that someday, whether you reject God or not, you will have to stand before Him in judgment. You will not be judging Him! The role reversal we have man-ufactured in this life is a façade. The reality behind it is that God, and only God, has the authority to judge. And He will judge everyone.

Avoid this disastrous error!

*Give God credit for being God. Spend time getting to know Him!

*Be thankful to your Creator. Your life has purpose in Him.

*Give God first place in your life and never give it away, no matter what!

*Be a truth seeker. Give God the worship He deserves!

*Consider time with God as time well spent. Be like His Son Jesus.

The truth is that God is opposed to the proud. In his heart the proud man doesn't care if God is opposed to him because he is hostile toward God. That's why it is so difficult for the truth about pride to penetrate the arrogant heart.

E! True Hollywood Story is a television show about actors, musicians and other stars' lives. Each story seems to have similar themes. The person becomes a star from humble roots. After stardom is achieved the humble roots are exchanged for a self-indulgent lifestyle that involves alcohol, drugs, sex and often a marriage or two that doesn't work out. Eventually the star's life comes crashing down. They end up spending years picking up the pieces. This is the 'I want to be like Nimrod' scenario played out in some-one's life.

Check out how God sees the pride-filled person:

- Proverbs 3:34 He mocks proud mockers but gives grace to the humble.

- Proverbs 16:5 The LORD detests all the proud of heart. Be sure of this: They will not go unpunished.

- Proverbs 18:12 Before his downfall a man's heart is proud, but humility comes before honor.

- Romans 12:16 Live in harmony with one another. Do not be proud, but be willing to associate with people of low position. Do not be conceited.

- 1 Corinthians 13:4-7 Love is patient, love is kind. It does not envy, it does not boast, it is not proud.

- James 4:4-6 You adulterous people, don't you know that friendship with the world is hatred toward God? Anyone who chooses to be a friend of the world becomes an enemy of God. Or do you think Scripture says without reason that the spirit he caused to live in us envies intensely? But he gives us more grace. That is why Scripture says: "God opposes the proud but gives grace to the humble."

The longer we get away with sin; the more confident we become. We begin to believe that we are either too smart to get caught and/or that everyone around us is not smart enough to catch us.

Moment of truth – you are not smarter than God!
You never have been and never will be!

ACTION POINTS

1. What is God's definition of pride? Read Romans 12:3

2. Since humility is the opposite of pride – what is God's definition of humility?

3. List 5 things you are thankful for:

4. Now say them to God!

❄ ❄ ❄

FOR SMALL GROUP DISCUSSION

1. Read the list of Scripture verses explaining how God sees the pride filled person.

- Proverbs 3:34 He mocks proud mockers but gives grace to the humble.

- Proverbs 16:5 The LORD detests all the proud of heart. Be sure of this: They will not go unpunished.

- Proverbs 18:12 Before his downfall a man's heart is proud, but humility comes before honor.

- Romans 12:16 Live in harmony with one another. Do not be proud, but be willing to associate with people of low position. Do not be conceited.

- 1 Corinthians 13:4-7 Love is patient, love is kind. It does not envy, it does not boast, it is not proud.

James 4:4-6 You adulterous people, don't you know that friendship with the world is hatred toward God? Anyone who chooses to be a friend of the world becomes an enemy of God. Or do you think Scripture says without reason that the spirit he caused to live in us envies intensely? But he gives us more grace. That is why Scripture says: "God opposes the proud but gives grace to the humble."

2. Discuss what each verse says about pride.

3. How can you avoid falling into the pride trap?

"I apologize for what resulted following an evening of celebrating the Super Bowl. I'm committed to being responsible and accountable, and apologize for my actions." Singer Randy Travis said.

The 52 year-old country singer was arrested for public intoxication early the Monday morning after the Super Bowl.

He was found drunk in his car with an open bottle of wine. He was parked outside of the First Baptist Church in Sanger, Texas.

Successful? Very!

Wealthy? For sure!

Fallen into an embarrassing sin? Yep!

Since Jesus died and rose from the dead; no one has to say, 'I've fallen and can't get up!'

Jesus is the one who lifts the fallen!

Chapter 3
The Roots of Stupid

Walter Payton was the great running back for the Chicago Bears in the 1980's. Payton could change the momentum in a game with his explosive speed, determination and quickness. He was admired by many. His nickname was 'Sweetness' and he was well liked and respected. Payton died from complications related to his battle with cancer on November 1, 1999. He was mourned throughout the nation. His funeral was attended by many notable people. He and his wife Connie started a charitable foundation to assist people with organ transplants. He was considered a sound family man as well as a man who cared about others. His reputation was sterling; until now.

Jeff Pearlman's recently released book about Payton's life is riddled with stories that do not flatter the great running back. One story in particular reveals the effects that sin has on you and those around you.

> "Payton was a nervous wreck on the day of his Pro Football Hall of Fame induction in 1993, because his longtime mistress had insisted on attending, and was staying at the same hotel as his wife Connie and children. The book says the two women talked after the ceremony, and Connie said, "You can have him. He doesn't want me or the children." USA Today 9/28/2011

Walter Payton could not enjoy receiving the highest honor a player can attain. As he addressed his adoring fans at the ceremony, his wife and kids were in the audience. His mistress was in a side room watching. His discomfort had to be intense! His sin put him in an awkward situation and he was found out.

Robert Robinson wrote the words to the great hymn 'Come Thou Fount of Every Blessing' in 1758. There are a couple of lines that speak directly to our daily struggles.

'Prone to wander, Lord, I feel it,
Prone to leave the God I love;'

The tendency to sin is a part of who we are as human beings. We possess a sinful nature that we cannot conquer on our own. Robinson captures this truth in the lines that follow:

'Here's my heart, O take and seal it,
Seal it for Thy courts above.'

We deal with the roots of sin in our souls every day.

John the Apostle explains, 'For everything in the world – the cravings of sinful man, the lust of his eyes and the boasting of what he has and does – comes not from the Father but from the world.' 1John 2:16

We have two enemies that work against us daily. One is an outside enemy the other is internal. The enticements provided by the outside enemy are designed by the evil one to give our internal enemy maximum impact. Let's talk about the internal enemy first because this is the battlefield closest to home.

John calls the internal enemy 'the cravings of sinful man'. We want certain things out of life for ourselves. When these things become the driving forces in our lives they are called 'cravings'. A craving is a strong desire. Cravings can be desires for things that are sinful in their design. An example would be a desire for cocaine – bad to the core.

Cravings can also be for things that are good in the right context but bad in the wrong setting. Sex in the context of marriage is great. Sex as pornography, adultery or in a premarital context is sinful. A good thing turned bad by aiming a desire in a sinful direction.

Money earned honestly and used responsibly is a great asset to a quality life. Money embezzled or earned in an illicit manner is sinful. 'The love of money is the root of all sorts of evil.' A good thing turned bad by a craving for more.

Sinful cravings are internal issues that each of us must clean up. But we are not left to do this on our own. While short term success may be possible through my own efforts; permanent change is very difficult to accomplish without help.

Addiction counselors tell us that recovery doesn't happen without openness and accountability. Addiction recovery groups generally connect you with a sponsor to hold you accountable and help during the times you are weak and ready to cave in to the craving.

Even if you are not an addict, these principles contain helpful advice. It is very helpful to share your problem with others who can support, affirm and encourage you through the difficult process of change.

Openness and accountability are keys to winning the internal battle.

Deciding to be open and accountable is a good first step in the process of removing the roots of stupid from your life.

Success or failure, however, depends on what you do next.

It is not enough to make the decision to change; you must follow it up with appropriate actions. Problem is; we often don't know what to do next. The spiritual and emotional energy involved in confession and sorrowful repentance is exhausting. That's why Paul tells the Corinthian church to come alongside the repentant person, affirming forgiveness and providing godly comfort (2 Corinthians 2:7).

How to follow up repentance effectively:

Step one: Go immediately to your pastor or an elder in your church. Privately share your story and have an honest conversation about your sorrow over sin.

Step two: Ask him to pray for you. You need strength to face each day. Request that he pray with you right now and for you every day.

Step three: Ask him to be your encourager and accountability person. Invite him to call and meet with you regularly. Give him permission to ask the hard questions required for recovery to occur.

Step four: Ask to meet with a group of elders to share your situation and ask them to pray over you.

> 'Is anyone among you in trouble? Let them pray. Is anyone happy? Let them sing songs of praise. Is anyone among you sick? Let them call the elders of the church to pray over them and anoint them with oil in the name of the Lord. And the prayer offered in faith will make the sick person well; the Lord will raise them up. If they have sinned, they will be forgiven. Therefore confess your sins to each other and pray for each other so that you may be healed. The prayer of a righteous person is powerful and effective.' James 5:13-16

I like the way the Holy Spirit inspired James to write this passage of Scripture. He names three situations that should move us to pray. We are to pray when we are in trouble, when we are happy or when we are sick.

If you have been caught up in sin; you are in trouble! So this instruction is for you.

The prayers of the elders will affirm your forgiveness and strengthen you. It also gives you a group of allies in your recovery process. Not to mention that this is one of the best things elders get to do!

Church Leaders Read This Carefully!

I am convinced that one of the key reasons people don't come to us is because they don't trust us with their hurtful and embarrassing stuff. Too often, we treat the repentant person like they were still in sin and need to be chastised. When someone comes repentant; they have already received forgiveness from Jesus. He does not use their sin as a club to beat them into submission. He doesn't have to! The truly repentant person is submissive to Jesus because that is the nature of repentance.

We must take the gentle recovery approach Paul talks about in Galatians 6:1:

'Brothers, if someone is caught in a sin, you who are spiritual should restore him gently. But watch yourself, or you also may be tempted.'

Life is messy! So helping the repentant person will be messy too! Remember, Jesus' cross was messy!

Here's what to do when someone sorrowing over sin comes to you:

Step one: Listen

Step two: Listen some more

Step three: Pray over him

Step four: Share Scripture with him that affirms forgiveness and recovery. (1 John 1:9)

Step five: Discuss a recovery plan. How often you will call and meet personally. This doesn't have to be elaborate. Just simply spend time together in God's Word as brothers in Christ who wish to sharpen each other.

Step six: Gather a few elders to hear his story, affirm forgiveness and offer encouragement. Remind everyone in the room of the importance of confidentiality. (Confidentiality should only be guaranteed as long as no one else is at risk in the situation and no crime has been committed.)

Step seven: Go with him to reconcile with anyone he has offended while caught up in sin.

WARNING: If you are a man meeting with a woman don't meet alone .... ever! The person you are helping is frail spiritually and emotionally. This causes a natural vulnerability to fall into other sins of the flesh. Paul says, 'Watch yourself, or you should also be tempted.'

If you are a man meeting with a woman make sure you have another godly woman in the room. Let her be the affirmation and accountability person – not you. Women should be helping women and men ought to help men. You can have the elders pray over a woman but make sure that all the follow up is done by a few godly women in the church.

The same practice is necessary when a woman meets with a man.

❋❋❋

I have some very old and very large trees in my yard. One in particular is scarred by the elements of Michigan weather. A piece of branch has broken off leaving a jagged edge. The trunk has been chewed on by who knows what. The bark is missing in a few places. In spite of all the imperfections the tree stands strong. Its strength comes from a well established root system. The same is true for you and me:

> So then, just as you received Christ Jesus as Lord, continue to live your lives in him, rooted and built up in him, strengthened in the faith as you were taught, and overflowing with thankfulness. Colossians 2:6-7

Whatever your root system is; it determines the strength and stability of your life.

A person who likes to lie sets up a root system that is shallow and a life that will fall over quickly. The liar thinks he is safe because he keeps adding more roots to his system. The problem is that none of the roots are deep enough to hold up to resistance. Many shallow roots do not add strength.

Good roots run deep!

A person who loves money sets up a root system that appears to be secure. Unfortunately, money only provides security from being financially strapped. It doesn't work very well at providing strength in your marriage or other relationships. Money can't replace time and attention. What may begin as a legitimate desire to be financially secure can turn into a lust for more. What seemed to be a good root goes bad and lacks the internal fortitude required to stay upright. 'The love of money is the root of all sorts of evil.'

Good roots are nourished properly!

ACTION POINTS

1. Read Colossians 2:6-7

2. Write out a few disciplines you can practice to keep you walking in the Lord.

3. What can you do to deepen your root system?

❋ ❋ ❋

SMALL GROUP DISCUSSION

1. What could you practice daily to be built up in Him?

2. What are the qualities of someone who is established in the faith?

3. Take some time to pray, expressing why you are thankful to God.

Sin Makes You Stupid
Part 3

Jesus is in the Recovery Business!

Actor Brad Renfro (The Client and Sleepers) and a pal were charged with grand theft after trying to take a $175,000 yacht on a joy ride. Catching them might have been harder if they hadn't forgotten to untie the boat, causing it to smash back into the dock.

-Stuff Magazine

Chapter 1

You are not stuck with Stupid!

Pat brought Chad to church after his wife kicked him out for drinking all the time. They came to talk to me after the service on that Sunday six years ago. The first thing Chad shared about himself was that he hadn't had a drink for almost two days. He was trembling nearly out of control and sweating profusely. I asked him to sit so he wouldn't fall over.

As he explained his situation and how he had messed up his life; I thought of three simple truths to give him.

The conversation went something like this:

'You have made some stupid decisions." Truth #1

'I know'

"You have also made some good decisions." Truth #2

'I have?"

"Yes, you decided to quit drinking. You decided to listen to Pat, a friend who has your best interests at heart. And you decided to come to Hillside today for church.'

'I guess those are good decisions.'

'If you keep making one good decision after another your life will change for the better.' Truth #3

'What should I do next?'

'Decide who you will allow to influence you and don't listen to any other voices.'

Chad chose his relentlessly godly friend Pat and me. Pat and I both recommended that Jesus be part of the team as well. Chad wasn't ready – Pat was relentless.

Pat called Chad's boss and convinced him to hold his job open while Chad went to rehab. During rehab Chad decided to make Jesus the key person on his life changing team.

Chad's transformation has been remarkable, painful and divine. If you ask him how long he's been sober he will say, 'I've been saved and sober for six years!'

His life is still hard. He is divorced. He spends time with his two children every week. He has been in and out of work for the past few years – like many in Michigan. But there's something about him that is strong and consistent. As God is transforming Chad he is becoming wise – a good decision maker. His struggles have made him appreciate his Savior. Now he has the soft spoken wisdom of a man who is walking through the obstacle course of life with God as his guide.

Chad has changed. He has gone from foolish to wise.

Pat and Chad are now on a mission from God. Determined to rescue their friends who are captive to sin.

If you ask Chad's best friend Pat why they pursue rescuing others. Pat will tell you, 'The devil isn't getting any more of my friends!'

These two former hell raisers are heaven bound and taking others with them!

Men transformed and living the adventure.

Life is tough but God is stronger!

The Apostle Paul explains what is happening to Chad in Romans 12:1-2

> I appeal to you therefore, brothers, by the mercies of God, to present your bodies as a living sacrifice, holy and acceptable to God, which is your spiritual worship.
> Do not be conformed to this world, but be transformed by the renewal of your mind, that by testing you may discern what is the will of God, what is good and acceptable and perfect.

Chad has been (and is being) transformed by God! Are you?

I love the Greek word for transformation – 'Metamorphosis'. One of the definitions of 'Metamorphosis' in the Miriam Webster Dictionary is: 'Change of substance by supernatural means'.

Those who trust Jesus are 'partakers of the divine nature' (2Peter 1:4). This is a huge change in your internal substance. You are now able to grasp how God thinks and live in the Wisdom Zone. The substance of your decision making has changed. Now you have input from the perfect, supportive and wise counselor Jesus.

This amazing life change has happened because of God's mercy received through His Son Jesus due to His death on the cross for our sin and His resurrection from the dead so now God has withheld His righteous hand of judgment and given us His amazing grace. I know this is a run-on sentence but sometimes it is hard to punctuate our praise!

Because of God's mercy you can now make good choices. Making good choices begins with getting the basic decisions of life locked down. The Apostle Paul covers the big two in the Scripture you just read.

Number One - Choose to present your body as a living sacrifice to God.

Now that you have received God's mercy; you are able to truly worship. This means that you can bring all of yourself before God, Who created you. The goal in worship is to have a life that matches your worship. If what you're giving to God in worship is not consistent with how you are living; your sacrifice is unacceptable. In order to present your body as a holy sacrifice you need to separate yourself from sin.

The evil one, society and your human nature all work together to squeeze you into conformity with sin.

Sin has its own value system. A system that both screams and whispers; demanding and enticing at the same time. A system designed to convince us that we have needs that God can not fill. A system that emits high decibel noise designed to make us sway to the rhythm of the evil one. The value system of sin wants us to choose conformity over metamorphosis. It compresses and manipulates us into taking on the shape of a system that opposes God's transforming work.

When sin's value system conforms you; you will sacrifice your body to it. Designed to project a 'harmless' image and to make God look like a spirit crushing ogre; sin's system wins you over.

Is consensual sex before marriage harmful? The 'system' wants to convince you that it is important to try things out before you make the big leap into marriage. Seeing if you are sensually compatible before you commit to a person for life. The problem with this thinking is that you sacrifice the external (your body) at the expense of the internal (sacred love).

God tells us to keep the marriage bed holy. He wants you to be regret free as you discover one another during your honeymoon and beyond. God knows that it's a great turn-on to hear your spouse say, 'I saved myself for you!' Marital love-making gives you a sense of security, trust, joy and intimacy you can't discover anywhere else. That's why statistics show that married people are more satisfied with their love-making than unmarried people.

Your Holy Spirit enlightened mind is able to think at an entirely different level than before. You have the 'mind of Christ', the ability to make quality decisions with a divine perspective. (1 Corinthians 2:6-16)

God always gets it right. Don't trade metamorphosis for conformity!

Number two - Be willing to be tested

Since we want to know God's will, we must adjust our lives to please Him. Paul guaranteed Timothy that anyone who desires to live a godly life can expect persecution. Jesus told His disciples that the world would hate us because we love Him. James says that we are to count the trials in our lives as blessings seeking to learn the deep lessons taught when we persevere under difficulty. Peter told believers that suffering through trials is like gold being refined in the furnace – but our faith is more valuable.

> Not only so, but we also rejoice in our sufferings, because we know that suffering produces perseverance; perseverance, character; and character, hope. And hope does not disappoint us, because God has poured out His love into our hearts by the Holy Spirit, whom He has given us. Romans 5:3-5

One clear aspect of your faith walk is to expect difficulty.

A deeper aspect is to accept it.

The truly intimate aspect is to welcome difficulties as valuable tests of our faith.

Job said that trouble is as common to man as 'surely as the sparks fly upward from a fire.'

(Job 5:7)

Expect difficulty.

Job accepted his extremely painful and impossible to understand trials.

"Naked came I from my mother's womb and naked I will depart. The LORD gave and the LORD has taken away; may the name of the LORD be praised." (1:21)

Amidst grief and incalculable anguish Job expressed the truly intimate aspect of his connection with God through his trials.

"I know that my Redeemer lives, and that in the end He will stand upon the earth. And after my skin has been destroyed, yet in my flesh I will see God; I myself will see Him with my own eyes – I, and not another. How my heart yearns within me!' (19:25-27)

Hope is stirred out of hardship. Hardship is used by God to stimulate an ever deepening intimacy in our walk with Him. You only get the intimacy if you welcome the tests!

Kyle was a good football player in High School. But not good enough to play in college. While still in high school, his dad decided that he wasn't improving because he wasn't being tested by the level of competition in his school league. Kyle went to football camp that summer. He was with the best players in the state.

After the first day he called his dad: 'These guys are really fast and really strong. I've never been hit this hard before!'

'Son, now you know what it takes to go to the next level. Are you up to the challenge?'

'Yes I am. By the end of the week I'll be playing even with these guys.'

He took the hits. His endurance was tested. His character was displayed. The life lessons he learned were beyond his expectations.

At the beginning of football camp he had some skill and a lot of courage. Now he is playing on his college team. He welcomes the new challenges freshmen players face at a higher level of competition. He looks forward to the test!

Are you willing to be tested?

Here's a Biblical self-test laid out in 1 Thessalonians 5:16-20

> 'Rejoice always, pray continually, give thanks in all circumstances; for this is God's will for you in Christ Jesus.
>
> Do not quench the Spirit. Do not treat prophecies with contempt but test them all; hold on to what is good, reject every kind of evil.'

'Rejoice always' is the theme that envelopes the rest of Paul's list. I have devised **Six Essential Tests** for every believer. These are daily challenges by which to test your-self. I recommend that you keep track of your progress. Measuring progress is important because it keeps you from neglecting one thing and over-emphasizing another.

This is a cumulative challenge. Accomplish #1 on Monday then add #2 on Tuesday. By Saturday you will be doing all six. Follow this pattern every week for six weeks. I hope you will discover that these tests will become a normal part of your life.

#1. Pray consistently. Take time to pray at the top of every hour. Nothing long; just simple and thankful.

#2. Be thankful in difficulty. Stop, look and listen. When you run into a difficult or frustrating situation today; stop and think about how to glorify God in the difficulty. Pay attention, looking for how God is using the difficulty to grow you. Listen for the Holy Spirit working on your con-science and in your heart, influencing you.

#3. Make the Holy Spirit proud! Don't quench His fire. Today, fan the flames of your faith and let God's warmth and love be known. Whatever the Holy Spirit puts on your heart today – do it now!

#4. Honor God's word. Think about some Scripture you have memorized and repeat it sometime during your day. Spend time reading your Bible. Give the Scriptures influential weight in your relationships and decisions.

#5. Cling to good. Affirm the good around you. When you witness someone doing good, tell them you appreciate it. Seek to do what God says is best. Let your integrity step to the forefront and be seen.

#6. Push away from evil. Filter your thinking through Jesus and His word. Be careful not to let yourself drift back to what you used to be. Change the channel. Watch your language. Guard your eyes and ears. Sanctify your imagination.

Now do your list again and again.

Soldiers go to Boot Camp to prepare for the battles they may fight in the future. Athletes practice constantly preparing for the contests they will compete in later. Students study in preparation for exams they will take soon. Prepare well. Welcome life's tests. Let God metamorphisize you!

ACTION POINTS

These are daily challenges by which to test yourself. I recommend that you keep track of your progress. Measuring progress is important because it keeps you from neglecting one thing and over-emphasizing another.

This is a cumulative challenge. Accomplish #1 on Monday then add #2 on Tuesday. By Saturday you will be doing all six. Follow this pattern every week for six weeks. I hope you will discover that these tests will become a normal part of your life.

#1. Pray consistently. Take time to pray at the top of every hour. Nothing long; just simple and thankful.

#2. Be thankful in difficulty. Stop, look and listen. When you run into a difficult or frustrating situation today stop and think about how to glorify God in the difficulty. Pay attention looking for how God is using the difficulty to grow you. Listen for the Holy Spirit working on your conscience and in your heart influencing you.

#3. Make the Holy Spirit proud! Don't quench His fire. Today, fan the flames of your faith and let God's warmth and love be known. Whatever the Holy Spirit puts on your heart today – do it now!

#4. Honor God's word. Think about some Scripture you have memorized and repeat it sometime during your day. Spend time reading your Bible. Give the Scriptures influential weight in your relationships and decisions.

#5. Cling to good. Affirm the good around you. When you witness someone doing good; tell them you appreciate it. Seek to do what God says is best. Let your integrity step to the forefront and be seen.

#6. Push away from evil. Filter your thinking through Jesus and His word. Be careful not to let yourself drift back to what you used to be. Change the channel. Watch your language. Guard your eyes and ears. Sanctify your imagination.

Now do your list again next week!

✳ ✳ ✳

FOR SMALL GROUP DISCUSSION

1. Read John 4:23-24

2. What does the phrase 'worship God in spirit and in truth' mean to you?

3. Read 1Corinthians 2:11-16 and discuss the positive aspects of having the Holy Spirit within you.

4. Contrast those who have the mind of Christ with those who don't.

5. Discuss the Cumulative Challenge from Action Points.

Which one is most difficult for you to do?

6. How were you blessed by doing the challenge?

Gregory Roberts, 43, of Las Cruces, New Mexico, was arrested at the public library shortly after 2 a.m. Tuesday, for breaking and entering. Officers found his shoeprints on broken glass where he allegedly entered by kicking in a window pane.

Once inside the library, Roberts got himself trapped between the outer and inner doors of the foyer. He couldn't get back in and he couldn't get back out. What could he do? He called police from a pay phone in the foyer. They got him out, but now Roberts is trapped behind another door: a jail door.

-Albuquerque Journal

Now he has lots of time to think about what went wrong!

He can think about the break- in or he can think about what went wrong with his life!

Chapter 2
Settle on your life direction

My wife and I were travelling recently to Lynchburg Virginia. I was using the navigation feature on my smart phone to keep us on track. We entered the Ohio Turnpike at Toledo and were settling in for the 100 mile drive before our next turn. Ten miles after we entered the turnpike the navigation system went berserk!

'Turn right in one quarter mile onto Marshall Road'

'Turn left in one hundred feet onto Lynch Avenue'

'Make a U-turn'

This went on for twenty minutes or so. I knew where we were. I knew that we were on the right road going in the right direction. The information I was getting from the navigator wasn't correct.

I turned off the smart phone; took out the battery for a minute. When I put the battery back in and rebooted the navigator worked well and has been fine since.

When you've made a series of poor choices in your life, it's time to reboot. Get your personal navigation system on line with God's will.

Since we know that God created us on purpose and with a purpose; we need to stay on His path for us. Remember that at the culmination of history everything will be measured by Jesus and through Him. That makes fulfilling His design for you an extremely high priority.

Live a life of presentation.

> Do your best to present yourself to God as one approved, a workman who does not need to be ashamed and who correctly handles the word of truth

> 2 Timothy 2:15

A mentor years ago told me, 'If it's not inspected it's neglected.' I have found this to be true in every area of life. Knowing that your life is being inspected by God gives you a great motivational advantage to do your best.

I am amazed that God is interested in me! He knows me completely and wants me to succeed in reaching my life purpose.

Appreciating how much He knows and loves me is strong motivation to do my best. To make God proud that He adopted me into His family.

Paul tells Timothy that he needs to be a workman who is not ashamed. Shame is a valuable asset in settling the direction of your life. Shame is part of God's quality control system for your conscience. We need shame to motivate us to correct the bad things we have done. Feeling shame for the right reasons tells you that your conscience is working and that confession and corrective action are required. When you choose to present your life as an offering to God, your conscience will call you to act accordingly. Settling the direction of your life helps you establish a sound criteria for measuring the spiritual quality of your life.

We are living sacrifices. Our lives are lived on the altar of God's will.

Seeking God's approval means that we must live in the context of His purposes. Living within the truth brings clarity and stability to our lives. God's direction becomes clearer as we walk by truth.

The Apostle Paul names two men who were not interested in living on the altar of God's will. They wanted to design their own belief system and spread spiritual poison among believers. Hymaneus and Philetus had wandered away from the truth – they chose not to live on the altar of God's will. Yet they wanted all the benefits of those who were living on the altar. Appearances can be deceiving. Paul's response to them is powerful and directed straight at the human heart.

> Nevertheless, God's foundation stands firm, sealed with this inscription, "The Lord knows those who are His," and "Everyone who confesses the name of the Lord must turn away from wickedness."

> 2Timothy 2:19

These statements can be either reassuring or terrifying depending on whether your life direction is settled with God.

'The Lord knows those who are His' is powerful in its implications. As you are reading this, God knows if you are really a believer or not. And you know it too! In a setting where the truth is clear, this is as plain as it gets. God knows and you know.

> 'The Spirit Himself testifies with our spirit that we are God's children.' Romans 8:14

If you truly want to settle the direction of your life with God; you can't get by acting like a Christian but not being one. If you are honest with yourself you know whether you are a believer or not. God's Spirit tells you. He does not want His children to be insecure. That's why He gave us His Spirit as His personal guarantee that we have life in His name. He is also our Guide while we walk through life as His children.

Those who really love God; living on the altar of His will are children in good standing. You know who you are!

Those who love God but have wandered off seeking sinful fulfilment are children in poor standing. Still part of the family but not living like it. These saints feel shame and guilt and experience God's discipline to bring them back into good standing.

> My son, do not make light of the Lord's discipline, and do not lose heart when He rebukes you, because the Lord disciplines those He loves, and punishes everyone He accepts as a son.   Hebrews 12:5-6

These are encouraging words for those who have wandered into sin. You know you are family when the Father disciplines you for your sin. The purpose of discipline is to teach you the foolishness of your wanderings, bring about true sorrow and restore you to right standing with the Father.

God is the perfect disciplinarian. His motives are always pure and effective. If you are being disciplined by God – you know it. If you are living a life of sin and not experiencing God's discipline, you may not be in His family.

People like to say they believe in God. Many like the idea of a heavenly Father looking over them. They think God is OK as long as He passively observes and only gets involved at their discretion. They attempt to convince themselves that they are believers. The truth is that they are not. It is spiritually deadly to toy with God's gift of salvation.

God is actively working all the time. He never sleeps. He is affirming, encouraging and correcting His children constantly. If you are His, you know it.

If you are not in His family; you need to be – now! Belonging to God is the key to settling the direction of your life.

Consider which of these prayers is appropriate for you:

- Lord, I love you! I am living on the altar of Your will. Thank you for giving me Your Holy Spirit to affirm and encourage me as I live for you.

- Lord I love you BUT I have put my will ahead of Your will in my life. Your Holy Spirit is bothering my conscience to get right with You. Forgive me for climbing off the altar of Your will. Thank you for correcting me. I'm back and I'm all in for your glory!

• Lord until now I have not been a believer. I live life my way, not Your way. I know now that Your way is the only way I can fulfil Your purpose for my life. I believe that Jesus died, paying for my sin. I also believe that He rose from the dead and lives forever. I ask You to forgive my sins because Jesus died for me. I ask you to give me eternal life because I believe Your Son rose from the dead. I want Jesus to be the leader of my life. I ask You to settle my life direction according to Your perfect and holy will. Thank You for making me Your child! I am now living on the altar of Your wil

Practice Spiritual Hygiene

Fifty high schoolers were milling around the church bus anxious to get going to our annual summer camp. The drive was long but no one seemed to care because the ride was part of the experience. The back of the bus was the area the kids went to talk, play games and hang out with the leaders. Early in the trip I noticed that most of the youth were crammed three to a seat in the front half of the bus. There was only one person sitting in the back. I felt bad for the girl alone in the back of the bus so I asked one of our more friendly teens to get some kids to go back and talk to her.

"Sorry Pastor Kevin, I can't help you with that.'

'Why not?'

"She smells."

"By the end of the bus ride we'll all smell. We're going to camp!' My voice dripped with sarcasm.

"You go back there and see if you can stand it. If you can I'll come too."

"Deal!"

I made my way to the back of the bus. When I was a few feet from the girl I was nauseated by the odor she was emitting. I was pretty sure she hadn't bathed – ever! It was bad but sad too. I went back forward and found my wife. I explained the situation to her and she headed toward the rear of the bus.

Her conversation with the girl revealed that she knew she smelled bad. She didn't think she had much value as a person and decided that rejection was going to be a way of life for her. Sheila explained that she was valuable to God and that she needed to live a life that reflected that. At our next stop, Sheila and our lady leaders helped her clean up. Before the week was over the girls in the group showed her how to make her hair look nice and other girl stuff.

She needed to learn about personal hygiene.

Every believer needs to learn about spiritual hygiene. The Bible calls it 'consecration'. Getting clean before God.

It is possible for everyone experiencing new life in Christ to let ourselves get dirtied by the world. We need to practice consistent consecration.

> Now in a great house there are not only vessels of gold and silver but also of wood and clay, some for honourable use, some for dishonourable. Therefore, if anyone cleanses himself from what is dishonourable, he will be a vessel for honourable use, set apart as holy, useful to the master of the house, ready for every good work. 2 Timothy 2:20-21

The vessel good for honourable use is clean.

When we eat we wash the dishes so they are clean for the next meal. We don't just scrape off the food scraps and put the dishes back in the cupboard. We are vessels for God's use and must keep ourselves clean so we are ready to be used.

We have been adopted by God the Father. We have the Right to call ourselves children of God! (John 1:12)

We have been redeemed by His Son, Jesus. Jesus, by the way, is our Creator. (Colossians 1:15-23)

We are lived in by the Holy Spirit of God. "God is our refuge and strength, a very present help in trouble." (Psalm 46:1). He wants to be so available that His Holy Spirit dwells within each believer! That's a close personal relationship!

We inherit what Jesus has.

> The Spirit himself bears witness with our spirit that we are children of God, and if children, then heirs— heirs of God and fellow heirs with Christ, provided we suffer with him in order that we may also be glorified with Him. Romans 8:16-17

We are related to the King of Kings! We belong to Him! We share His eternal kingdom!

We have nobility!

Express your nobility!

Paul tells Timothy to keep himself clean because he is used by God for noble purposes.

- Express your nobility by giving people directions to the glorious Kingdom of Jesus!

- Express your nobility by acting as God's ambassador to your part of the world and beyond.

- Express your nobility by modelling the gracious and generous character of our King. (Galatians 5:22)

- Express your nobility by pushing away from evil and avoiding sinful temptations.

- Express your nobility by coming into the throne room of the King to talk with Him every day.

Write your own expressions:

Express your nobility by _____

Express your nobility by _____

Express your nobility by _____

Express your nobility by _____

Express your nobility by _____

Living in the context of the nobility we have in Jesus motivates us to consecrate ourselves. The responsibility for daily cleaning is on us. 2Timothy 2:21 tells us to 'cleanse ourselves'. God makes us holy when we come to Christ but it is our duty to clean off the daily dirt.

Timothy needed pictures to lock in his mind in his faith walk through life. Paul gave him three in 2 Timothy Chapter Two. Each speaks clearly of God's expectations.

The first is a soldier who keeps himself from worldly entanglements so he is ready when his commander calls him into battle (:3-4).

The second is an athlete who prepares with discipline, anticipation and obedience. He has a strong desire to win the race by competing according to the rules (:5)

The third is a diligent farmer who plants with the harvest in mind. He works well ahead and is patiently consistent while watching for growth every day :(6-7).

Nobility requires a higher level of expectation from ourselves. We need to get our priorities in line with our nobility and live for our Father and His Son, our King.

Cleansing calls us to sorrow over our sins, confess and live obediently. The best you can ever be is who you are in Christ! You only get there through consecration.

Spiritual hygiene is critically important because it reflects how we view life.

Joshua was the new leader of Israel. Moses had died and now it was Joshua's calling to lead the Israelites across the Jordan River into the Promised Land. They had hiked through the wilderness for forty years because they did not believe God's promises. But now they were one day away from going in. God gave Joshua instructions. Joshua directed his leadership team who in turn directed the people.

In the midst of all the anticipation; Joshua gave an order to the Israelites:

"Consecrate yourselves, for tomorrow the LORD will do amazing things among you."

He calls them to make sure their spiritual hygiene was right. Cleaned up inside and out.

Upon reading this verse I had to ask myself a very hard question. It took a while to answer because I didn't want to admit my failures to myself.

How many times has God been ready to do amazing things in my life that I have missed because I was not con-secrating myself?

I challenge you to give much honest reflection to this question. If you are like me; it will break your heart and change the way you think about spiritual hygiene. It will also change the way you look at your life. I have been much more observant to God working in and around me.

I'm noticing things I never saw before!

I have a renewed sense of the nobility I have in Jesus.

God used the breaking of my heart to open it up so I can receive more of Him.

Tough challenge – great outcome!

Keep moving!

> 'So flee youthful passions and pursue righteous-
> ness, faith, love, and peace, along with those who
> call on the Lord from a pure heart.'

> 2 Timothy 2:22 ESV

Settling the direction for your life means that you have to get moving and keep moving! When an athlete runs a race, the further he gets from the starting line the closer he is to the finish. He runs away from one thing while running toward the other. I call this the Perseverance Distance Principle because the race we run as believers demands perseverance. A champion doesn't quit when he begins to tire or faces obstacles; he presses on. Fleeing the starting line as he strives to finish well.

Timothy's mentor tells him to flee and pursue at the same time. He is to flee youthful passions – those strong sinful desires that can dominate our lives if we let them. By the way, 'youthful passions' don't only affect the young. We are effected at every age by our own lust!

God tells us to ambitiously pursue four distinct objectives. We are to be accompanied by others who are pursuing the same ends. It is critically important in our pursuit to run with like-minded people. I'm not talking about people who simply say they have faith. Or those who think their faith walk is like strolling through the park on a sunny day. I'm talking about people who share your passion for the pursuit of godliness. If we want to flee successfully from evil passions; we must be passionate in our godly pursuits.

'Passion' is the key element to pursuit. Passion is the factor that causes us to go on when the run is uphill. Passion is the drive that motivates us to get up when we have fallen and are badly bruised. Passion fuels the joy of teamwork as we strive ahead tired, sweaty and yet exuberant!

Our passion is supercharged by the One who calls us to **The Pursuit**. You must know, however, that there are strong implications attached to each of the four aspirations listed:

Righteousness means making choices and decisions that are right with God as the key priority.

Faith has to do with trusting Jesus by submitting in obedience to Him every step of the way.

Love feeds you the energy that keeps your stride fresh and crisp. The energy comes from receiving God's love as a natural part of your life. Only when you receive His love can you give it out. The stride in your faith walk is the output of love received. Get this right! If you are not receptive to Jesus' love continually you will be attempting to run on your own power. Exhaustion, anxiety, guilt and a nagging sense of inadequacy will weigh you down because you can't manufacture Jesus' love – you must be open to receiving it. That's where the joy comes from. Jesus said, 'Love one another even as I have loved you.' Our ability to give love is directly related to receiving His love!

Peace is achieved when your conscience is in alignment with God's will. The Holy Spirit lets you know when you're drifting out of alignment. Plugging Scripture into your mind is God's recommendation for managing your conscience.

"How can a young man keep his way pure?
By guarding it according to your word.
With my whole heart I seek you;
let me not wander from your commandments!
I have stored up your word in my heart,
that I might not sin against you.
Blessed are you, O Lord;
Teach me your statutes!
With my lips I declare
All the rules of your mouth.
In the way of your testimonies I delight
as much as in all riches.
I will meditate on your precepts
and fix my eyes on your ways.
I will delight in your statutes;
I will not forget your word."

Psalm 119:9-16

A friend of mine wrote this in her statement of faith in Jesus:

"Life has a way of wearing you down if you don't stay grounded in the LORD." (Beth Wooster)

ACTION POINTS

1. Write your own expressions of the nobility you possess in Christ.

I express my nobility by _____

I express my nobility by _____

I express my nobility by _____

I express my nobility by _____

2. Think about God's purpose for your life. Can you define it?

If not, ask Him to help you see it by noticing your strengths and the opportunities He puts in your path.

✳ ✳ ✳

FOR SMALL GROUP DISCUSSION

1. Discuss ways that life can wear you down when you drift away from God.

2. How do you think someone can discover God's purpose for their life?

A woman was at the pharmacy picking up a prescription for her daughter. When she returned to her car she discovered that she had locked the keys inside.

As she looked around, she spotted a coat hanger on the ground. She knew that people broke into cars using coat hangers but had no idea how they did it.

Feeling helpless, she prayed, "Lord send someone to help me!"

Within a few minutes a leather-clad, bearded, tough looking man pulled up next to her on his motorcycle. He dismounted and walked toward her.

Still feeling helpless, she prayed, "Lord protect me from this man!"

"Can I help you?" he asked.

"Yes, I am locked out of my car and only have this coat hanger. Can you use it to get me into my car?"

"Sure" He opened the door in less than a minute.

She was so relieved that she hugged him, "Thank you, thank you! You are such a nice man!"

"I am not a nice man. I just got out of prison today. I was locked up for car theft." He smiled and walked into the store.

She prayed, "Thank you God for sending me a professional!"

Chapter 3
Be Yourself in Christ!

You can only be your best self when you are in Christ. Jesus said, 'Abide in Me and I in you.' That means we walk, talk, move, think and feel our way through life enveloped in Jesus. I picture myself living in a bubble that surrounds me as I move through life. The bubble is the context of my life. That's me abiding in Christ.

The bubble also permeates me completely – through and through. It influences my thoughts, feelings, attitudes and decisions. It fills me with a true sense of security; reminding me that I am constantly loved with the best love there is. This part of my bubble is Jesus abiding in me.

I am filled with Jesus and surrounded by Him at the same time. He's the only one who can do that – He's God!

We are each created on purpose with purpose. Both are determined by our Creator.

We are each born with abilities, intellect, personality, creativity, physical traits and skills. All of these and yet we are incomplete.

Incomplete but with the capacity to know God. The Westminster Catechism states, 'the chief end of man is to worship God and enjoy Him forever.' Every person no matter how talented, good looking, intelligent or creative is incomplete without Jesus.

When you realize that you are incomplete and lost without Jesus, you should immediately turn to Him for forgiveness and set Him up as the King of your life. Jesus explained this to Nicodemus by saying,

> "Truly, truly, I say to you, unless one is born again he cannot see the kingdom of God." Nicodemus said to him, "How can a man be born when he is old? Can he enter a second time into his mother's womb and be born?" Jesus answered, "Truly, truly, I say to you, unless one is born of water and the Spirit, he cannot enter the kingdom of God. That which is born of the flesh is flesh, and that which is born of the Spirit is spirit. Do not marvel that I said to you, 'You must be born again.' The wind blows where it wishes, and you hear its sound, but you do not know where it comes from or where it goes. So it is with everyone who is born of the Spirit." John 3: 3-8

When you are born again you become a complete person. The elements of completeness are only given to those who are born of the Spirit. These elements define who you were created to be.

You are a son!

> But when the set time had fully come, God sent his Son, born of a woman, born under the law, to redeem those under the law, that we might receive adoption to sonship. Because you are his sons, God sent the Spirit of his Son into our hearts, the Spirit

who calls out, *"Abba,* Father." So you are no longer a slave, but God's child; and since you are his child, God has made you also an heir. Galatians 4:4-7

You have been adopted by God and now have all the rights of sonship.

The right to call God your Father.

The right to an inheritance in the future.

You now have legal standing as family with God the Father. He seals (guarantees) our standing through His Spirit living in us. The verses above use the terms 'Abba' and 'Father' to describe sonship. The first is a familiar term letting us know that God cares about our sorrows, struggles, joys, victories and defeats. He is the Father who embraces us and empathizes with us as we live the purpose-filled adventure of life we were created to experience. The second term is formal, keeping us mindful that we are under His protection and guidance. His power umbrellas our lives giving us peace in the raging storms.

Along with the rights of sonship, God gives us each spiritual gifts that compliment His creative purpose for our lives. Each of us receives spiritual gifts specially designed to complete us as individuals. These gifts are to be used for the good of God's church. Blessing those who are already part of the family and attracting those who are not.

You are a representative!

You now represent the King of Kings. You are not only adopted into His family but you are now a citizen of His kingdom. One of the great benefits of citizenship is that we get to represent our awesome and amazing King! Paul told the Corinthian believers that they were Jesus' ambassadors. We belong to Jesus and live as 'sent ones' to bring His news to the world.

> Therefore, we are ambassadors for Christ, God making his appeal through us. We implore you on behalf of Christ, be reconciled to God. 2Corinthians 5:20

I like to look up word meanings so I don't misunderstand what I am being called upon to do. The Apostle Paul says that 'God makes His appeal through us' and 'implores' us to be reconciled with God. If I am to live as a representative of Jesus I must know what God means when He 'appeals' through me. I also need to understand what he means by 'implore' so when I implore people I don't mess it up.

Appealing has to do with coming alongside someone and inviting them to listen to God. There are many ways to do this and God leaves it up to us (guided by the wisdom of His Holy Spirit) to decide how to represent Him to each person. We can represent Jesus by comforting the hurting, by encouragement, by issuing a challenge or a warning or by pleading with someone to accept God's invitation to know Jesus. Remember that the message of God is paramount no matter which approach you use.

When we **implore** someone it means that we want something very badly and we want it now. There is a great sense of urgency to God's appeal. It is very important. Why is it important? Look at the next statement Paul makes:

For our sake he made him to be sin who knew no sin, so that in him we might become the righteousness of God. 2Corinthians 5:21

As citizens of Jesus' kingdom, we have the privilege of being representatives of reconciliation.

You are a Friend!

"Greater love has no one than this: to lay down one's life for one's friends. You are my friends if you do what I command. I no longer call you servants, because a servant does not know his master's business. Instead, I have called you friends, for everything that I learned from my Father I have made known to you. You did not choose me, but I chose you and appointed you so that you might go and bear fruit—fruit that will last—and so that whatever you ask in my name the Father will give you. This is my command: Love each other."

John 15:13-17

Jesus expressed many things with His disciples at the Last Supper. His followers were troubled by what they heard and had difficulty absorbing it all. They didn't actually get it until they talked with Jesus after His resurrection.

As they left the Last Supper and walked to the Garden of Gethsemane, Jesus talked to them about friendship. He said, 'I am the Vine, you are the branches.' He wanted them to grasp the connection He has with us. A connection that is life-giving. A branch not connected dies on its own. The vine provides all that is necessary for life. Jesus is telling them and us that we are connected. A connection so necessary that Jesus states, 'Apart from Me you can do nothing.' Your life purpose cannot be realized without connecting to Jesus!

The connection is based on His love for us. A deeply personal sacrificial love that supersedes all other love.

"Greater love has no one than this, that someone lay down his life for his friends." John 15:13

He defines this connection by calling us His friends.

The character of our friendship with Jesus is based on our common purpose. The purpose is to glorify the Father through our relationship to His Son. We do this by bringing fruit to the table. Jesus tells us that His Father is the Gardener and trims the branches to increase the bearing of fruit. This is an uncomfortable process but very worthwhile. God wants us to develop the fruit of a godly character. We receive a package of Holy Spirit fruit upon salvation. The list is found in Galatians 5:22-23;

love, joy, peace, patience, kindness, goodness, faithfulness, gentleness and self control.

Nine types of character fruit given to each believer. Each of us has them all. The Father prunes the branches (us) to cause us to mature in each area. The impatient believer may be pruned in such a way as to make him learn to use the fruit of patience in his life. It is there already but must be developed. The self gratifying believer needs pruning to develop the trait of saying 'no' to self and 'yes' to God. That's self control – it's there already – but not mature.

You may be half the person you should be! Only in Jesus can you be complete!

ACTION POINTS

1.   What areas of your life is in need of an infusion of 'smart'? (God's wisdom)

2.   Take time each day to ask God to give you His wisdom for that particular area of your life.

3.   Who do you have in your life that gives you wise counsel?

4.   Let that person know that you appreciate them and tell them why.

Now, go live smarter!!!

❋ ❋ ❋

FOR SMALL GROUP DISCUSSION

1.   What have you learned from this book? Be specific about how what you have learned changes the way you look at your life.

2.   How will it help you live for Christ?

epilogue: I taught my children not to use the word 'stupid' in their conversations. But after serving in ministry for a few years I realized that sin makes smart people do stupid things. I began using the phrase 'sin makes you stupid' in sermons and counseling sessions. People who heard me speak began repeating the phrase to their friends. Everyone seems to laugh when they first hear it. Then they say, 'Wow! That's really true!'

My daughters are grown, married and have children of their own. They began encouraging me a couple years ago to write a book titled, "Sin Makes You Stupid!" So I did!

I hope this book helps you to live smarter!

May God show you when temptation is coming your way.

May He give you the wisdom to see it for what it is.

May He endow you with the courage of Jesus to say, 'NO!'

May He lead you daily in His everlasting ways!

28033626R00085

Made in the USA
Lexington, KY
07 December 2013